Negotiate Like A Villain

Practical Multi-disciplinary Negotiation tactics that dominate every time

Table of contents

1. Life as a series of negotiations
2. The meaning of negotiation
3. The competitive traits of man and the instinct to win
4. The importance of negotiation
5. My earliest memories of negotiation
6. Types of negotiation
7. BATNA (Best alternative to a negotiated agreement)
8. How relationships influence negotiation
9. What type of a negotiator are you?
10. Basic skills to have as a negotiator
11. Meet the Villain
12. The tactics of mind games
13. Strategies and tactics of a villain negotiator
14. Emotions and body language during negotiation
15. Responding to threats during negotiation
16. How to win business negotiations
17. Real estate negotiation
18. Relationship negotiations

19. Negotiations in marital discord
20. How to win public auctions
21. Tactical and practical salary negotiations with employers
22. Dealing with counter reactions during salary negotiation
23. Salary negotiation mistakes to avoid
24. Negotiation skills for career women
25. Crisis negotiation skills (Business crisis, robbery, hostage, violence)
26. Negotiating with terrorist organizations and organized crime
27. Government and political negotiation
28. Lessons from International Negotiations and noted strategies
29. The psychology of mass protest as a tool for negotiation
30. Law court negotiation
31. Exercise to take before a negotiation/conclusion

LIFE AS A SERIES OF NEGOTIATION

Ordinarily, there isn't much about life and its caprices that juxtapose it with a bed of roses, but of course, in life, you can choose to have a single stick of rose, a bouquet, a bed of it, or just stick with the little thorns on its stalk; it all depends on how hard enough you negotiate. Our everyday life is stringed by a series of negotiations, some, so subliminal that we barely even notice the efforts we've put into negotiating as we glide through, while others keep us right on the edge and push us into the deepest spate of anxieties. As though we were on a chessboard, we plan so many moves ahead, we do not think only of our moves but we summon a foresight of the next move of our counterparts. We gauge the fairness of what others want from us compared to what we want from them because this is how life works - everybody wants something, and life is a competitive field.

Villains, most venerably, love to get whatever they want and to the very magnitude, they want it. So, in listening to what the opponents say, we encounter demand, and we place our desires at the forefront, always. If life isn't always fair, we want to be on top and not the bottom, and like the calculative game of chess; we find vantage points and go for the jugular. We win or at least we try hard enough – in totality, we try to win more than we lose. Nobody in life ever wants to lose...ever.

Too often, people set goals too high and some too low, neither is good for negotiations. What happens in such instances is that they do not get through with the deal or they get through with far lesser value than they anticipated (buyer's remorse). Statistics have proven that most people do better in negotiations when they set optimistic but realistic goals and hang on to them, but most importantly, they cancel out the odds surrounding too-high goals by implementing the perfect strategies.

Negotiation is a life skill, it occurs often in our career lives such as splitting office tasks with colleagues at work, discussing initial salaries and raises with employers and employees and it spills into the most mundane of our daily activities like quick morning talks with spouses over house bills and chores, urging kids over their homework and general demeanor, with the promise of minor rewards. In short, a plethora of things to be negotiated, spring into our faces without warning. Some of these negotiable situations leave us with little to no time to make the right decisions and negotiate wisely, for instance when we negotiate in the face of sudden danger and with the potential of parting with a valuable thing such as our lives, our emotions, and brain work under pressure and depending on the severity of the situation, we fall into a state of panic that distorts our intellectual composure and shrewdness. Therefore we require the skillset and confidence of a villain negotiator to maneuver our way into winning in every situation.

To understand how to negotiate like a villain, we must be aware of the personality tweaks that follow – ultimately, people's strategy of negotiation goes along with the personality they choose to wear in order to get what they want, so this skill doesn't necessarily have to be innate; not everyone is born a good negotiator but everyone can learn. When it comes to negotiating complex situations, personality is power. In subtle ways, your attitude impacts your negotiation outcomes, for instance, the impatient man finds negotiation one of the hardest skills to learn, certain people are so impatient that they walk away too soon, rather than persist and push through, they easily exhaust, get irritable or despaired, therefore they miss out on so many deals in life, from small to big. We've also hinted that the most powerful negotiators are not intimidating personalities but charming personalities because likeability makes things a lot easier, for instance, in negotiations, people typically feel better giving up things to people they like, while people who are aggressive and termed bullies leave doubts in the minds of people, which in turn makes them lose more deals than they win.

Remember that every negotiation of importance will have some obstacles and you ought to prepare your mind to withstand them by following the best strategies.

"In business as in life, you don't get what you deserve, you get what you negotiate."

- Chester L. Karrass

Opportunities to negotiate

The moment I snoozed my alarm clock a third time from its scolding ding, my conscience revolted; I felt it in the way I lost the urge to go back to slumber. I was forced to get up from the small-sized bed in my little dingy room to prepare for a private meeting with a potential client. It was supposed to be a formal but cozy meeting. I was the host and I needed to win over his heart and cancel all doubts about being the man for the job because I wasn't going to charge pennies, so I decided to pinch out of the small cash in my wallet to lodge in a mini hotel suite; the cheapest suite there was, and there I can play the well-off host and bargain with squared shoulders. I wasn't a fan of living a lie but the world has rules; people create the first impression by the way you present yourself and in the way you host them, so my choice to lodge was like an investment, I needed my potential client to place a higher value on my worth and yield to my negotiations.

This hotel was nice and had a variety of rooms according to class, there was the luxurious suite that my budget forbids, there was the average, which would take a lot from me and there was the simple suite, the only one I could afford, so I checked in. I had prepared myself for the negotiations with my client; his first email had read that from my profile, I wasn't up to the standard status to have his contract, and perhaps that was why I decided to go through all this pain.

I looked around the simple hotel suite, it was tidy and fine, nothing really impressive. I stepped into the bathroom and was met with the surprise of my life; there was a dead mouse on the floor, possibly freshly dead, and was yet to stink up. I grimaced disgustedly, left my room, and went straight to the hotel lobby, I thought about laying my complaints to the receptionists and I guess they would apologize and ask me to hold on so the caretaker could clean up, I didn't make any complaints at the reception, instead, I demanded to see their manager, and they yielded to my request very shortly.

The manager was a lithe man with friendly eyes. I spoke with him congenially, I introduced myself as a journalist/blogger and businessman and he sized me up with his eyes without further hesitation I told him what I had encountered in the bathroom of my suite and I explained that I was expecting a meeting urgently in case they were thinking of sending over a caretaker to clean up. I had to mention this just to cancel out the option.

"Oh very well my friend, do tell them at the reception to give you another suite by my orders." I stared at him silently, and then I asked "what kind of suite would it be?"

He shrugged, "What kind of suite were you lodged in?"

I smiled and said to him "You know, my profession as a blogger makes life more interesting because in life you always have a little story here and there to tell when you feel dissatisfied." I was looking straight at him. There was a sudden brood in his eyes, like that of a threatened mouse; he didn't want anything that wasn't good for the image of his business.

He rubbed his chin and tilted up his head lightly "Of course, since this is a compensation, sort of," he reasoned, "One of the luxury rooms will be prepared for you immediately, I think you would like that, wouldn't you?"

"That's better." It was an automatic upgrade; those luxury suites were expensive as hell. When I walked into the luxury suite they had prepared for me, I felt like a king. Asides from the fact that I knew I would thoroughly enjoy my stay and I would boast about having tasted the luxury suite which I ordinarily couldn't afford, I have a potential client who is concerned about gauging my success in a bid to be sure that he wasn't dealing with an incompetent, desperate man who was after enriching himself with his money. So when I place big bargains and drop sizable quotation prices on the deal, he would as well be able to negotiate with higher perceived value on my status, with the thoughts that if I could presumably afford this expensive luxury suite, then I was likely worth what I say I am.

I could tell by how the negotiation kick-started, that he took me more seriously than when he had first emailed, and our negotiation went according to my expectations.

So many people in my shoes would not see an opportunity here and if I was like them, I could silently go back to a cleaned-up room, and at most I would tell my friends about it later or wallow in silent dissatisfaction about the incautiousness of the hotel staff. If I had complained at the reception, they would have apologized and possibly extended it to a written apology by the management which was a total waste of my time and theirs, but negotiating subtly yet menacingly, for better treatment like I feel I deserved – since the compensation was within their capacity and they had absolutely nothing to lose – was a win-win. In short, if it had been a more delicate issue like consuming something that was potentially harmful to my health, my quick-thinking self would have had greater demands, of course, even monetary compensation. I had negotiated my way into preparing a better picture for the bigger negotiation.

THE MEANING OF NEGOTIATION

Before we get down to the basics, negotiation itself must be deeply understood – It can be defined as the dialogue between entities that aim to reach a consensus on issues of shared interest. The goal of negotiation is to obtain an agreement on one or more contentious issues between two or more parties. The deal may be advantageous to all or some of the participants. To improve their prospects of closing deals, preventing conflicts, developing connections with other parties, or maximizing mutual benefits, the Negotiators should determine their own needs and wants while also attempting to understand those of others involved.

A villain negotiator is daunting but at the same time builds trust; such a person isn't necessarily aggressive or violent while negotiating but has a quick thinking capacity and charm to relay his intent. The villain negotiator also has self-confidence and a spirit others often yield to. The level to which the negotiating parties trust each other to carry out the negotiated solution is a major determinant in the success of a negotiation and villains are the party that is quick to find your fears and leverage them, depending on the situation at hand they minimize or maximize it while making their offers.

The premises of negotiations can take place anywhere at all – either one-on-one or virtual, in which case, as you read along, you will learn to pick the best environs to negotiate, depending on the nature of the situation at hand.

Public organizations, including companies, non-profits, and government, sales and legal proceedings, frequently engage in negotiations, as well as private situations like marriage, divorce, parenthood, friendship, etc. Expert negotiators often have a niche. Union negotiators, leverage buyout negotiators, peace negotiators, and hostage negotiators are a few examples of professional negotiators. They might also go by different titles, such as brokers, legislators, or diplomats. Automated negotiation is the practice of conducting negotiations with the use of algorithms or machines; this is usually used in professional fields. The participants and process must be accurately characterized for automated negotiation; an example of this is in sponsored search auction, where bids are placed on advertisement keywords.

THE COMPETITIVE TRAITS OF MAN AND THE INSTINCT TO WIN

The human mind is highly competitive and are bedeviled with the fiery desire to get ahead of others. Perhaps we should blame it on evolution—our genes increase our chances of survival and procreation, and competition is key to both.

We live in a materialistic society because asserting our control and amassing wealth and other material things elevates our social position. High-status individuals are able to attract high-status partners, increasing the likelihood that their immediate offspring and extended generation will survive.

The brain rewards us with serotonin or dopamine just for attempting to elevate our status (such as during a competition or sporting event) commonly referred to as "brain chemical rewards". Every emotional impulse, unless we improve on this perception, is rewarded and this includes being cruel, bullying, intimidating, showing off, getting angry, yelling, striking out at other people because they all show dominant behavior, and this tells that there is a villain in everybody, we choose when to activate this villain mode.

The 1.0 version of the human operating system is what has been described above. We find that the primitive stage of mankind and child form has little to no control over these inherent dominant traits. For instance, a child shows a crude temper and throws tantrum immediately if things don't go his or her way, they are yet to get a grip of their emotions. You become version 2.0 of the human operating system if you can manage your emotions. You will have a much wider range of alternatives for how to react to the outside world. You'll develop into a far more intriguing and unpredictable person. Your brain will reward you if you can resist making domineering displays, elevating your rank above the majority of people on the planet.

So, the insatiable desire to compete can be attributed to a few things, firstly, all living things have that as an inherent, inalienable quality. Life is robust, active, adaptable, and advanced because of it. Because those who didn't compete with others in their species ceased to exist, every living thing has an innate urge to do so. In ancient times, winning meant surviving or having a chance to copulate and have descendants. This raw animal instinct is clearly demonstrated in the Serengeti, the jungle shows us the nature of man when survival and procreation are of utmost priority.

Also, we always desire to win simply because winning makes us feels better, be it a kind of sport or competition, and even when no one is watching us; during the games, we play in private, we still want to win. As though life itself was a game, we always keep trying to break the high scores our friends make because it gives us the confidence that we are better at something, and why not? In the society we live in, winners get more attention and are honored while losers are treated the opposite way. It is the winner who always gets an award and an elevated sense of reputation.

During an interview, Kris had tagged himself a serial winner.

When I asked what his motivation in life was he said it wasn't "success" because success was a vague term, but when he broke it down to the actual things that he wanted from being successful, it made more sense, and he said:

"I don't know about other people but I want to live and I want to win, simply because I want to see things, places and women that will make my heart stop; beautiful, exotic things. I want to have the best wine and the most exotic food at my disposal. I want to be able to afford the most expensive things and then chose not to buy them because I don't exactly need them, and I want to be rich enough to magnet the best caliber of men and the most gorgeous women towards me. It would feel good to have the world know my name. Lastly, while I live my best life, I want to make memories, lasting memories that I will happily cling to and feel satisfied with, even on my deathbed.

Some other guy, Liam with a simpler dream went a little blank for a while when I asked what his motivation in life was. I realized that he was like so many people out there; they weren't quite clear on what motivates them in life. In a quest to simplify my question I asked "why do you wake up each morning?" I hoped that was narrowed down a bit, but I realized that this was one of the times when oversimplifying made matters more complex. He did respond "I wake up each morning because I have to go to work, and the reason I go to work is that I want to get paid. I want to afford my bills and expenses so I work for money."

He was as "present-thinking" as possible, he didn't have a motivation outside of his immediate lifestyle and he was like so many people I know. They just need money to fund their simple lives, hand them a good wad of cash and they will keep off from work only to get more hours of sleep and relaxation since they do not have to report to the office.

In understanding humans and their urge to win, I've also come to realize that there are people who want to win as they want others to win equally, the win-win model and there were others committed to the win-lose model, these are aggressive competitors anyone would dread to negotiate any deal or situation with. In my experience, these are often people with fragile egos: they are only briefly satisfied with having won. They're very soon desperate for the next victory. And losing isn't just something that happens on occasion: it's usually felt as evidence of a deep and shameful personal flaw.

Most of us have a passion of some sort—something in which we want to excel at. Of course, we strive to "win" in that area, but we're usually content to compete in other areas for the sheer pleasure of the game. We accept the occasional failure as part of the learning process although we would sincerely like to win all because we consider winning highly reinforcing and strongly connected to our self-esteem.

THE IMPORTANCE OF NEGOTIATION

So someone's going to think "hey most of us aren't high-powered attorneys or corporate dealmakers, we are just everyday people. Why do we need to be expert negotiators?"

The crazy thing about life which we've all come to accept is that it's really good at pitching, and many times, its favorite sports balls are lemons. Wellington whose daughter had been kidnapped had no idea he would be bargaining and negotiating the life of his only child a week ago while he was at the cinema laughing with a mouth full of butter-caramel popcorn.

Rodriguez whose mortgage was long overdue and faced with repossession had no idea that if he talked his way into getting that big loan, he could offset his mortgage and he would own a house, convert a part of its space into a B&B and purchase his dream Labrador.

Learning negotiation strategies, dispute resolution, and overall communication skills is a vital part of becoming a well-rounded person who can commendably advocate for themselves in the workplace or any place or situation they find themselves. Honing your negotiation skills and becoming an effective negotiator is a must regardless of your field; this is because people who don't negotiate frequently are typically compelled to negotiate with experienced negotiators.

For instance, you typically have to bargain when you buy a car.

It may be the first time you've bargained in weeks, months, or even years for yourself. It's likely the eleventh negotiation the salesperson has had that day. This occurs frequently in both the business and personal worlds. Negotiating a salary is never enjoyable. The price of a product is typically negotiable when going up against a skilled negotiator.

The importance of negotiation can't be overstated. A good Negotiation strategy is often the secret to getting ahead in the workplace, adding value to contracts, and resolving conflicts.

When disputes arise in business and personal relationships, maneuvering your way around them, through apt negotiation skills, helps in avoiding escalation and saving the relationship.

Nevertheless, it is also possible to turn unpleasant disagreements into productive negotiations and retain solid connections. In these circumstances, bargaining abilities are very crucial.

In a few capsules, here are the importance of negotiation in our lives:

1. To maximize satisfaction

Satisfaction is the cornerstone to any negotiation process, more so than the money or products we might acquire from it. We bargain in a way that satisfies the interests and desires of both parties (win-win negotiation). Both parties in a negotiation look for their own satisfaction in addition to any actual benefits that may come from the process (money, services, ego, competition, security, etc.). The greatest barrier to satisfaction is that it is a subjective idea and thus impossible to quantify.

Something that may make one person satisfied might leave another person dissatisfied, the stage of information exchange and attentive listening is crucial in this situation because of this. During that time, we can learn what truly satisfies our conversation partner while also providing some hints about our own wants. Satisfaction cannot be traded. The villain, like anyone else who likes the idea of winning, is always unable to trade mutual satisfaction. In other words, neither you nor the other party may insist that the other party relinquish to your satisfaction.

We may not deeply assess the satisfaction of others but we can get hints from their body language, and tone, whether verbal or written.

One of the biggest threats to satisfaction is the rush to make the first concession, it greatly lowers the satisfaction rate during a negotiation win-win. The first step in learning how to bargain is to maintain composure and refrain from acting rashly. For instance, imagine that you have been upholding your word for hours, repeatedly promising that there is no room to cut a product's price. If you abruptly lower the price significantly, your credibility will suffer since your spouse will feel deceived even though you are, by definition, trying to make them happy. This tactic might be used against you in upcoming talks.

2. To foster relationships

One of the indisputable fundamentals of negotiating is to establish a long-term relationship, work cooperatively, and create agreements that are advantageous to both parties. Positive negotiating relationships are crucial because they foster trust, which is a crucial component of getting others to do what you want them to.

In building a relationship, try to discover your negotiation counterpart's hidden interests. Build a relationship in negotiation by asking questions, then listening carefully to assess your counterpart's interests with sufficient empathy in order to stimulate honest responses.

According to social science studies, people frequently act similarly to how others act. We tend to reciprocate in kind if people work with us and treat us with respect.

We are more prone to act defensively and aggressively ourselves if they appear to be doing so. Positive communication during a negotiation can also lead to cooperation and general goodwill.

3. Crisis Management

This requires an extra skill to water down tension, bitterness, and all forms of negative emotions that are stirred during a crisis, whether it is in a business environment, housework, or any public office. Negotiation tactics are deployed to make parties involved in the crisis in order to reach a consensus. We see this during riots, robberies, hostage situations, business-deal-gone-bad, etc.

4. To extract unexpected value

While trying to purchase some fishing paraphernalia from the fishing company we had patronized for almost half a year, I suddenly said to the guy in charge of sales "You know what, I don't think this is worth the money, we ought to be paying only 80% of what you charge." I stifled a smile. My second, Owen, nudged me, it was some silly joke I was putting out, so he thought, but I was half serious. The guy in charge stood there for a while, I wanted to say to him "Never mind." and have him help us carry the things into the truck like we always do so I can settle the bills but he surprised me when he said, "That's no issue if that retains our most valuable customer."

Owen had wanted to tell him it was a joke but I prodded him to stop. I was thinking about how quickly he had agreed and how we had paid an extra 20% all this while, I felt cheated and I wanted to suggest to our superior that we stop purchasing from their company entirely, but when I did my research, I found that they offered the best prices and his agreeing to the 20% slash was out of benevolence. Now we saved 20% of our expenditure on fishing materials, there goes the power of negotiation to extract unexpected value.

5. To capitalize on opportunities

Negotiation brings forward opportunities but we ought to be very realistic with our targets. For instance, having seen how impressed my new employer was with my performance and job interview, I took the opportunity to slip in a request that could help me get more leisure on the job; while on the negotiation table for my remuneration, I brought up the issue of "vacation time". To be frank, I was willing to go ahead with the job if he had turned down my request, but I sort of knew that these people wanted me for their organization. My request was immediately granted and that also opened the door to a new office yearly routine for everyone as well and I was glad I had brought that into the negotiation.

6. To avoid hidden dissatisfaction and its later problems

Even if you were in a higher position of authority and you know that you could have a bigger piece of the pie if you wanted, and without any consultation, you may get to take your opponent into consideration because he/she may be openly or secretly dissatisfied. You could have things your way and face the fight that would sooner or later result, or you could avoid that and go for a peace agreement that favors involved parties by negotiating.

An example of this situation is the strike by teachers in Chicago:

Rahm Emanuel, the former chief of staff for President Obama, alienated Chicago schoolteachers after becoming mayor of the city in February 2011. For example, he reneged on a pay raise promise and lobbied the Illinois state legislature to restrict the issues the Chicago Teachers Union (CTU) could bargain and go on strike over.

A 10-day strike was called in mid-2012 as a result of unsuccessful contract negotiations between the CTU and the City of Chicago. In the end, a deal between the CTU and the school board was struck, and this resulted in gains for both parties, including a longer school day and yearly teacher salaries.

It can be tempting to try to make choices on important matters individually when a confrontation is imminent because you worry that negotiations with the opposing side will fail. Although this tactic might be successful in the short run, it's crucial to consider the long-term costs of a backlash. The example of Emanuel demonstrates that tough fighters are not always successful negotiators.

7. To settle disputes and bridge divide

It takes negotiations to have multi-tribal nations as we do in some parts of the world today, each tribe has a representative that speaks on behalf of his people and in order to ensure governance that brings unity and keeps the different tribes together despite their various wants and agitations, it takes the efforts of tactical negotiation on a topmost level, and when disputes arise from differences, those in the position to negotiate will settle the disputes amicably.

MY EARLIEST MEMORIES OF NEGOTIATION

When I was just 9 years I used to go to the open markets with my mother to get some meat and vegetable, I realized quickly that when I went on the same shopping with my dad, it took only half the time it did with my mother, and here's why: my father was a simple man, once he needed an item and he had the right amount of money for it in his wallet, he didn't waste time placing too many bargains. My dad would take a shot at bargaining only when he had been told an obviously exorbitant price for what he wanted to buy. My mother was a lot more of a vicious negotiator; she would negotiate till she got the very last penny she could save out of that purchase. She dedicated her time, and she walked out on so many offers, unrelenting and she would meet more than ten people dealing in the same item just to get the very best price out of all of them. She negotiated with them one after the other till they either yielded to her desired price or they got impatient and told her off, sometimes, the sellers lost their temper and got aggressive and yelled at her but she would quietly make her way to the next seller of the same item to begin another negotiation. For me it was intriguing and at the same time, I always had to prepare for sore feet from moving from one person in the market to the other, right beside her. After all these years, I am yet to meet someone who was a more ardent negotiator than she was.

I watched her conversations long enough to realize her strategy: whenever she was told the price of an item, she takes it as just an opening price with a lot of potential to shed value, she considers it grounds to initiate a counter bargain as viciously as one who is at the brink of being robbed. After all, it was only the stinky rich who wasted money in paying up at the opening offer. So what she did at her first counter bargain each time, was to slash the price into half and place her bargain price a little lower than a half. For instance, if someone told her something costs $40 dollars, she asked to purchase it for $16 dollars for starters. For a product she already knew the price range, she tried to get the lowest minimum price that can be paid for it.

I had also watched her potential customers, when their reaction was a natural surprise or an expression of dismay, I guessed that my mother had gone way lower than the actual value of the item, whereas if the seller's reaction was mild or indifferent, then there was a very good chance that my mother's price was still within a fair range no matter how low she had gone, this also implies that the seller had given a cut-throat initial price and was out to rip her buyers off a large chunk of money for profit.

One thing I admired was my mother's composure, the reaction of the sellers didn't matter to her, she was immune to their grumpiness, irritability, and impatient body language, and she only had her eyes on the price I had started to think that it was an act she relished in because of how much time and patience she dedicated to it, best of all, she had never lost her patience, she had never bantered words to an angry customer, it was a sell-it-or-leave sort of poise she negotiated with—extremely void of emotional attachments.

At the end of the day, we went home with two full grocery bags without having spent so much and when we placed the items on the table my dad's eyes would bulge in astonishment, he would jokingly ask "Did you go shopping today with a gun in your handbag?" and we would laugh about it.

All these years, I couldn't help but notice that my mother always wore the most beautiful clothes I have ever seen whenever we went out and she matched them up with expensive jewelry, bags, and shoes. I got a bit curious because I had barely seen my dad give her money for her personal shopping; neither did she have any income. It was then I decided to find out "Where do you get the money to buy all these, does dad give it to you?" I said to her one day. She looked at me and smiled and replied "Your dad and I struck a deal when we got married. Whenever he gave me just the adequate amount of money to buy raw food and household items at the market, he tells me, you can keep the change if you had a good bargain." It was then I realized why she bargained so rigorously. She proudly said to me "The change that you keep could be small or big, it all depends on how hard you negotiate." I quickly understood everything as I nodded at her admiringly. I knew someday I would grow up to become a good negotiator, if I would be as good as she was or better, I didn't quite know.

CATEGORIES OF NEGOTIATION

Firstly, negotiation fall under two categories, distributive negotiation and integral negotiation

1. Distributive negotiation

A type of negotiation known as distributive negotiation, sometimes known as zero-sum negotiation or win-lose negotiation, is one in which one party wins only if another loses. A distributive negotiation typically entails talking about just one topic. For instance, a sales company might seek to sign a contract with a vendor of IT services. The business wants as many IT services as it can get at the lowest cost, but the IT vendor wants to offer the fewest resources at the highest cost. A distributive negotiating strategy is one where both parties are motivated to seek a better bargain.

Here are some pointers for winning a distributive negotiation:

- Be tenacious.
  Persistence and courteous firmness can help you advance your interests in a negotiation when you use a distributive strategy.

- Make the initial move.
  You can present the first offer in a distributive negotiation to start the negotiations in your favor.

- Keep your minimal favorable outcome a secret.

To achieve successful negotiation in distributive talks, it's critical to set high goals. When negotiating for the finest outcomes, you can keep any information about the very lowest you're willing to accept a secret.

2. Integral negotiation

This is also known as win-win negotiation or collaborative negotiation, it is a negotiation strategy in which the parties to the discussion work to find a solution that benefits both of them. Integrative negotiations can include a variety of topics, unlike distributive negotiations.

For instance, a well-known fashion brand and a new cosmetics business decide to work together on a product aimed at their respective target markets. They work out a deal that will help the fashion company meet its financial and marketing objectives while also giving the cosmetics upstart more visibility.

Following are some pointers for an integrative negotiation:

- Embrace moral principles.
  In order to establish confidence with the opposite side during an integrative negotiation, you can talk about your principles.

- Openly express your demands and interests.
  In an integrative negotiation, discussing your objectives can increase transparency and foster a good working partnership.

- Use negotiation to reach a resolution.
  In an integrative negotiation, both sides can utilize the process as a chance to work together to solve problems.

Four different types of negotiations

1. Honorable negotiation

A style of bargaining known as "principled negotiation" uses the principles and interests of the parties to come to an agreement. Conflict resolution is frequently the main focus of this kind of negotiation. In order to advance the interests of both parties, this kind of bargaining employs an integrative negotiation strategy.

Four components make for a principled negotiation:

i. Gain for all parties: The integrative strategy for a moral negotiation encourages participants to concentrate on negotiating solutions that will benefit both sides.

ii. Focus on interests: In principled negotiation, parties can recognize and express their goals, points of interest, and needs.

iii. Distinguish emotions from the topics: During a principled negotiation, participants can lessen emotional reactions and personality conflicts by concentrating on the pertinent issues rather than how those issues make them feel.

iv. Objectivity: In a negotiation based on moral principles, the parties can agree to use objective standards as a starting point. Market pricing, professional judgments, legal restrictions, and industry norms are a few examples of objective factors in negotiations.

For instance, the managers of two departments in a major corporation frequently disagree about how much funding should go to each department. To find a solution, the two leaders engage in a principled negotiation. They consider each other's arguments before deciding to base resource distribution on the proportion of sales that each department contributes to the overall company.

The two department heads compromise by agreeing to support the operations of the other department, which has more resources.

2. Group negotiation

Multiple persons negotiate on both sides of the negotiation in a team negotiation. Large corporate transactions frequently involve team talks. On a negotiation team, different personality types play different roles. In some circumstances, one person may play multiple roles. The following are a few typical jobs on negotiation teams:

Leader: Each team in a negotiation typically elects a leader to render the final judgments throughout negotiations.

Observer: During a negotiation, the observer pays close attention to the team representing the other party and shares their observations with the leader.

Relater: During negotiations, a relater on a negotiation team tries to establish rapport with opponents.

Recorder: A member of a negotiating team who is tasked with recording discussions during meetings can do so.

Critic: Although this position may seem unfavorable, having a critic on your team can assist you to comprehend the concessions and other unfavorable aspects of an agreement.

Builder: A member of a negotiation team that builds the

agreement or package for the other side. They are able to handle financial tasks like assessing the cost of an agreement while negotiating.

3. Multiple-party negotiation

A multiparty negotiation is a sort of bargaining in which more than two parties are involved. A huge company's negotiations with various department heads are an illustration of a multiparty negotiation. The following are a few difficulties that multiparty negotiations face:

> i. BATNA
>
> BATNA stands for "best alternative to a negotiated agreement" and refers to changing BATNAs. A negotiation involving numerous parties can make it more difficult for the parties to come to an agreement because each party's BATNA is more likely to vary. At every point of the negotiation process, each party can assess their BATNA to determine the outcome of a proposed agreement.
>
> ii. Coalition formation
>
> The potential for different parties to establish coalitions or alliances presents another difficulty in multiparty discussions. These partnerships may make bargaining more difficult. To assist all parties in coming to a consensus, coalitions can settle on a certain set of conditions.
>
> iii. Problems with process management
>
> The management of the negotiation process involving numerous parties may result in poor governance and misunderstandings. By selecting a leader who is prepared to work with others to reach a compromise, participants in multiparty discussions can steer clear of these problems.

The Settlement for Mortgage Foreclosure in the US is an example of the problems with multiparty:

After months of challenging negotiations, the attorneys general of 49 states and the Obama administration came to an agreement with five of the largest banks in the country in early February 2012 with the intention of stabilizing the housing market in the United States and punishing the banks for abusive foreclosure practices.

The agreement was applauded by several observers as evidence that the nation was starting to recover from the housing crisis. Others, however, criticized it for just assisting a portion of the affected homeowners. This illustrates how challenging it is to strike a balance between many objectives in complicated multiparty conversations, even for renowned negotiators. This problem could be solved by improving communication and bargaining within each party individually.

4. Competitive negotiation

A distributive strategy called combative negotiation allows the most aggressive side to get an agreement that advances their goals. Here are a few illustrations of antagonistic negotiating strategies:

- Hard bargaining: In a hard bargaining tactic, one party refuses to make concessions in order to reach an agreement.

- Future promise: In this strategy, the opposite party is promised a benefit in the future in exchange for current concessions. By demanding the future promise in writing, you may combat this strategy.

- Loss of interest: Loss of interest is another combative negotiation strategy in which one side says they are no longer interested in negotiating a deal.

BATNA

(Best Alternative To A Negotiated Agreement)

BATNA is a very important word in the world of negotiation and we must fully understand what it means and how to use it. The best alternative to a negotiated agreement, also known as BATNA (no deal option), is the most advantageous course of action a party can take in the event that negotiations are unsuccessful and an agreement cannot be reached. The BATNA might cover a variety of circumstances, including the execution of strikes, switching to a new negotiating partner, appealing a court's decision, transitioning to another negotiating partner, and forming other types of alliances. [1] A successful negotiator has their BATNA as their primary focus and motivation. In general, a party shouldn't consent to a resolution that is worse than its BATNA. The value of the connection, the time value of money, and the chance that the other party would uphold their end of the bargain should all be taken into account when appropriately valuing deals, it should be noted. Since they typically depend on hazy or qualitative variables rather than those that are straightforwardly observable and quantifiable, these other considerations are frequently challenging to value.

Often, it is much more challenging to ascertain the BATNA of the opposing side. However, because the BATNA establishes the opposite side's negotiating strength, this information is essential. A person's primary interests can sometimes be used to deduce conclusions, and the negotiation itself can be used to confirm or refute the assumptions. Setting a later delivery date on purpose can be suggested, for instance, if it is thought that the negotiating partner places a high priority on a very early delivery date. The targeted delivery date is probably going to be very important if this late delivery date is categorically denied.

When no player can gain from switching strategies if every other player maintains their existing strategy, a set of players has attained a Nash Equilibrium. For instance, if Amy is making the best choice she can while considering Phil's choice and if Phil is making the best choice he can while considering Amy's choice, then Amy and Phil are in Nash equilibrium. Similar to this, a group of participants is in Nash equilibrium if each is making the greatest choice possible while also taking into account the choices of others.

Negotiators frequently view BATNA as a source of leverage in discussions rather than a safety net. The evaluation of a negotiator's alternative options ought to be simple in theory, but frequently no effort is made to determine which option best represents a party's BATNA. To be useful, alternatives must be real and implementable, but without the time investment, options that fall short of one of these requirements are routinely included. Most managers underestimate their BATNA while spending insufficient time investigating their actual possibilities. As a result, decisions and negotiations may be made incorrectly or poorly. Additionally, negotiators must be informed of the opposing party's BATNA and assess how it differs from their own.

Some people might use forceful, coercive, threatening, or even dishonest tactics. This is referred to as a "hard negotiation style" – an adversarial approach style negotiation is an example of this in theory. Others might choose a soft approach, which is affable, trustworthy, accommodative, and conflict-avoidant. When harsh negotiators and soft negotiators meet, hard negotiators typically prevail, but at the risk of possibly deteriorating the parties' long-term relationship.

To create a powerful BATNA, appealing alternatives are required. Here are three ideas for how to do this:

1. making a list of possible steps to pursue in the event that no agreement is reached
2. turning some of the more attractive ideas into concrete and partial alternatives
3. the best-sounding alternative should be chosen

All parties in cross-cultural discussions must take cultural cognitive behaviors into account and refrain from letting assumptions or biases interfere with the negotiation process. This is just to make the parties to the negotiations aware. Also, preparation at all levels, including bias-free ideas, emotion-free conduct, and actions, is highly beneficial to the process.

BATNA-based strategies and flow of negotiation

Numerous strategies aim to undermine the opponent's BATNA since it is crucial for the success of the negotiation. This can be done, for instance, by attempting to have exclusive negotiations, postponing or speeding up present negotiations, or restricting the negotiation partner to technological systems. If a negotiator encounters such techniques, it is his or her responsibility to assess the potential effects on their own BATNA and to stop or reverse any worsening of their own party's BATNA.

The BATNA may also affect the sequence in which talks with possible contractual parties are initiated. A sequential strategy is preferable. When using a sequential strategy, one begins talks with the less advantageous partners and then moves on to the more advantageous choice.

A contract with the least advantageous party is hence the BATNA.

BATNA and reservation values are different.

A reservation value indicates the worst offer any party is ready to accept, whereas a BATNA represents one party's best choice should discussions fail. Never allow a reservation value to be less than the BATNA. The BATNA might stand for the choice to shop at a different dealer while buying a bike, for instance. The reservation value would be the most you would be willing to pay, based on the cost of locating alternative vendors.

The procedure for creating the best substitute for a negotiated agreement

- List all potential alternatives to the current negotiation first – what would you do if it ended in failure?
- Establish the value of each option by calculating how much each one means to you.
- Select the choice that will be most beneficial to you (this is your best alternative to a negotiated agreement)
- After finding your BATNA, calculate the lowest-priced offer you're willing to take.

Three different kinds of BATNAs exist:
1. Walk-away BATNA
2. Interactive BATNA
3. Third-party BATNA

Walk-away BATNA

The buyer will walk away and choose the other alternative if the vendor won't lower the asking price to make it less expensive. Researchers and professional negotiators both view the BATNA, or "walk away," outcome as the main source of a negotiator's relative power. However, relying on substitutes carries some risk. The ability to employ resources to affect another party's circumstances is a sign of one party's relative power in a negotiation, and the importance of a BATNA in this context can range from important to nonexistent.

Interactive BATNA

When one or more parties in a negotiation are not working with the other parties, interactive BATNAs are needed. The three most common interactive BATNA types are as follows: [14]

Economic example: If a newspaper forgot to replace an improper ad in one issue, 50% of its subscribers would cancel their subscriptions, costing them half of their advertising revenue. The unwilling party in this scenario would be the unsubscribers.

Political: An illustration would be one political party voting down a bill that another party is attempting to pass. The party filibustering in this situation would be the uncooperative one.

Social: An illustration would be a gathering of protesters that resisted police attempts to scatter them. The uncooperative party in this scenario would be the protesters.

Third-party BATNA

When two parties in a negotiation are unable to reach an agreement on their own or their disagreement is unresolvable, third-party BATNAs are sought. So, a third party is needed for the purpose of:

Mediation: A neutral third party is enlisted to assist

the conflicting parties in coming to a mutually acceptable resolution through. The conflict is not resolved during mediation; rather, it is merely facilitated.

Arbitration: A neutral third party is involved to settle the dispute by intercession or a BATNA. They find a solution, as opposed to the method of mediation.

Litigation: When negotiations go south, the law steps in as an authoritative third party, and the matter is resolved in court with both parties being required to abide by the ruling.

HOW RELATIONSHIPS INFLUENCE NEGOTIATION

The impact of relationships on negotiations is sometimes undermined, they can be very impactful. Ever considered why you would want to build a rapport that will influence your negotiating counterpart to yield? That's simply because relationships influence decisions during negotiation a great deal.

Below are the kinds of relationships in negotiation

- Business-Only Negotiation
- Friends-Only Negotiation
- Mixed Negotiations

Fundamentally, negotiating is an exercise in interpersonal communication. The manner in which the negotiators communicate and the bond that develops have a significant influence on the negotiation process. For instance, research shows that communal-sharing relationships increase empathy and cooperation in negotiations, improve decision-making and performance-coordination tasks performance, increase attention to the results of the other party, reduce the use of coercive tactics, increase the likelihood of information sharing, and increase the likelihood of compromise and problem-solving approaches to negotiations.

Negotiation is frequently used to learn more about the other side and deepen interdependence rather than to discuss a specific problem. Connection preservation may be the purpose of some talks, and in order to maintain or strengthen the relationship, the parties may make concessions on important points.

Relationship negotiations might go on forever. To get the negotiations off to a good start, parties may postpone discussions on difficult matters. Issues that the parties genuinely disagree on might never be resolved. It's frequently impossible to try to predict the future and discuss everything upfront.

Business-only negotiations

Because the expectations for the partnership are clear and concise, negotiations in business-only relationships are unusual. Market pricing is a standard tactic in business discussions. This is a way of valuing things that allow for the comparison of numerous qualitatively and quantitatively different aspects by reducing everything to a single value or utility metric.

In a blended or friend-only relationship, market pricing is challenging. The need to swiftly build trust in a circumstance where there is little knowledge or prior contacts is a major challenge in a commercial transaction. Furthermore, status and rank difficulties are frequently present in commercial partnerships.

Example of business only negotiation:

Social media platforms like Twitter and Facebook do business according to utility metrics and numerical figures the customer and transactions are based on ads and user data so negotiations on pay and evaluation are strictly business-like. In another instance, Swash a web3 data service that allows its users to monetize the value of their data when they allow companies have access to it. These customers become numerical figures and are measured in utility metrics rather than as people and their identity is narrowed down to their data.

Friends-Only Negotiation

Friends-only negotiations suffer from a number of drawbacks that make them more challenging. Most people find it awkward to bargain with friends. Cultural and exchange norms contribute to some of this discomfort.

Taking care of those we love and are close to, attending to their needs, and not keeping account of who has contributed to what in the relationship are cultural norms that drive us. The giving and taking of resources and benefits is governed by exchange norms. Friends are therefore frequently less competitive with one another.

The issue is that friendship can prevent people from reaching highly integrative agreements. When resolving a dispute, friends frequently lean toward equity or equality norms. When friendship results in the improper handling of an agreement, this is a phenomenon known as the "Abilene paradox."

Example of friends-only negotiation:

After Paul confides in his friend Fred about how he gets retail sneakers extremely cheaper than other sellers and gets off a neat 100% profit from the general market price while the other sellers make 50% profit, Fred wants a pair of sneakers from his friend at a much lesser price. Fred calculates a 50% profit for him only willing to negotiate for a discount less than Paul usually sells. Paul will eventually consider his friend's request despite his financial targets.

Mixed Negotiations

An embedded relationship is a partnership between two parties that has both personal and professional aspects (such as friendships or family ties). Sticky bonds are relationships that result from deeply rooted patterns of prior social encounters.

In mixed discussions, there is a significantly increased risk of emotions, internal value conflict, and a lack of originality or inventiveness.

So you are about to enter into a negotiation with a counterpart, these are the questions you need to answer on a sheet of paper, to understand your standpoint in the game play and tie loose ends.

- Do you have any kind of relationship with your counterpart in the past or present? (Proceed with the rest of the answer is Yes)
- What sort of relationship do you have with your negotiation counterpart?
- How do you think your relationship will affect the negotiation dynamics?
- What do you think would contribute to the presence of trust in your negotiation?
- What rational do you have and what deliberate methods can be used in building trust in this negotiation?
- What are tendencies that could lead to mistrust and how can it be fixed?

Example of mixed negotiation:

Excessive familiarity began to happen in my business due to constant patronage by same customers and my friendliness to in order to retain them, but then again, it wasn't long before "boundaries began to be crossed" especially with my customers in proximity. For instance, my customers, Wendy and Rachael, run the coffee shop beside me. I have breakfast there almost every day and I was able to convince them to use my hair salon. Now they waltz in and get a hairdo with a promise to pay in two weeks or whenever they deem convenient. I'm tempted to have a bargain with them to get free coffee everyday till i reach the value of their credit, even though I would have preferred my cash in hand. I wish they hadn't turned partial friends.

-Tina

Trust in negotiation

The reciprocal nature of trust emphasizes the importance of spending the time to get to know the other person and establish rapport before you start to negotiate; therefore relationship building is a necessary component of negotiation as well.

Don't believe that you can establish a connection with someone just by sending them a few cordial emails before you meet in person when trying to build relationship pre-negotiation. Instead, make an effort to develop a personal relationship by scheduling a few informal lunches.

Building relationships is vital for success in business, politics, security, and other areas. It is known as "Guang-Xi" in Chinese (Relationship built over time). Of course there are suggestions that it is employed in unethical ways. A problem with buying influence does arise occasionally, yes. Building relationships is crucial for negotiation, but caution must be exercised to avoid going too far. Building relationships is a key to success, I've discovered from my involvement in numerous negotiations and consulting projects. Trust is crucial, but you should exercise caution throughout the process because time and results will speak for themselves.

Whatever its base, wise leaders, like competent negotiators, try to build a strong connection since effective leadership actually depends on it. A relationship in negotiation is a perceived link that can be psychological, economic, political, or personal.

It appears that "schmoozing" (talking to someone in a friendly and lively way in order to impress and manipulate them) and other methods of rapport-building can have a considerable positive impact on business in addition to fostering trust.

WHAT TYPE OF A NEGOTIATOR ARE YOU?

Most element of our life is impacted by our ability to bargain, from establishing limits in our personal relationships to agreeing to a commission pay rate. Our success and well-being can be significantly impacted by how we handle interpersonal interactions. To determine what sort of negotiator you are and whether you need to develop that type in different scenarios, you should be aware of your own style.

There are five different negotiation approaches or strategies. These five tactics, which are based on the dual-concern concept, have frequently been discussed in literary works. According to the twofold concern model of conflict resolution, people's preferred means of resolving disputes are focused on two themes or aspects.

    i.   A concern for self (assertiveness)
    ii.   A concern for others (empathy).

On the basis of this paradigm, people strike a balance between their own wants and interests and the needs and interests of others. Depending on an individual's tastes and whether they have pro-social or pro-self aims, they can use one of the following five styles. These styles are subject to change throughout time, and certain styles may appeal to different people more than others.

1. Accommodating:

This category takes pleasure in maintaining interpersonal relationships and resolving disputes with the other side. Accommodators are perceptive to their counterparts' verbal cues, body language, and emotional states. However, when the other side doesn't put much attention on the relationship, they could feel exploited. Conflict can be handled pro-socially and passively by offering accommodation. Giving in to others' demands allows people to resolve both significant and little disputes. They sometimes retract after realizing the flaw in their argument and accept the position others have taken. However, in other circumstances, they could give in to pressure or group unity and drop all criticisms even when they aren't genuinely persuaded that the opposing side is right. Therefore, giving in might signify either sincere conversion or feigned obedience.

2. Avoiding:

People who take to this style dislike negotiating and won't do it until necessary. Avoiders tend to postpone and avoid the aggressive aspects of negotiation, but they can come across as polite and considerate. A passive strategy for resolving conflicts is inaction. Conflict avoiders adopt a "wait and see" mentality in the hopes that issues would go away on their own. Conflicts are frequently tolerated by avoiders, who do nothing to reduce their intensity. People that rely on avoidance tend to alter the subject, skip meetings, or even quit the organization altogether rather than discussing problems directly. Sometimes people simply decide to part ways. Individuals who like negotiations that require coming up with novel solutions to complex issues. Negotiations are a wonderful way for collaborators to learn about the problems and goals of the other parties. A proactive, pro-social, and pro-self approach to dispute resolution is collaboration. People who cooperate understand the problems that underlie the disagreement and then cooperate to find a resolution that is acceptable to both parties. This approach, which is also known as collaboration, problem solving, or a win-win approach, encourages both parties to the conflict to take their adversary's outcomes into account as well as their own.

3. Competing:

This is for people who take pleasure in talks, since they offer a chance to gain something. Competitive negotiators are often strategic and have excellent instincts for all facets of the negotiation process. Competitive negotiators frequently overlook the significance of connections since their approach has the potential to dominate the negotiation process. Competing includes enforcing one's point of view on others and is an active, pro-self method of handling disagreement. In order to scare others, those who employ this method frequently view disagreement as a lose-lose scenario. Fighting (forcing, dominating, or contesting) can take a variety of different forms, such as authoritative command, challenges, arguments, insults, accusations, whining, retaliation, and even physical violence. All of these techniques for resolving disputes are contentious since they entail forcing one's answer upon the opposing side.

4. Compromising:

This style is for people who are eager to reach an agreement by acting in a way that is equitable to all parties participating in the discussion. When there is little time to close the transaction, compromisers can be helpful, but they frequently hurry the negotiation and provide compromises before it is necessary.

The villain negotiator can use one or all of the above styles of negotiation except the compromising option, depending on what the goal is. He/she would "accommodate" their adversary's perspective just to win over their trust and make them think they have their best interests at heart. Villain negotiators would also "avoid" the conflicting part of negotiation if there are hints that there might be deal-spoilers down that lane. They "compete" in order to dominate if they have to and impose their bargain on a perceived weaker counterpart. They never "compromise"; they always have their eyes on the goal.

The three voices of negotiation

The differing approaches and presumptions of categories of negotiators are broken down below. Which one best captures your voice? Are you passive, aggressive or assertive in your negotiations?

Passive Negotiator

A passive negotiator prefers to always give way to the wants of the other person rather than expressing their own needs. When they do communicate their own viewpoint, they frequently feel bad about it and over-explain it. This kind of negotiator prefers to lose than handle conflict and will do whatever to avoid it.

Passive negotiators frequently consider:

"I'm a horrible negotiator" - yielding to defeat before they've even started the process

"I don't know if I deserve this," - Being an advocate for oneself is really challenging when you feel unworthy.

Imagining conflict and then trying to prevent this imagined conflict: "I don't want the other person to become furious if I ask for too much" (at their own cost).

Aggressive Negotiator

Negotiators who are aggressive adopt a "take-it-or-leave-it mentality" when engaging in any exchange. They typically demand for prompt replies since they have very little patience for deliberation. They frequently employ emotional manipulation, such as blame, shame, and guilt, to acquire what they want instead of stating their wants honestly.

Aggressive negotiators often think:

"Screw them before they screw me," they're assuming that everyone will try to trick or treat them.

"Nice people always come last," implying that being fair and considerate is a sign of weakness.

Assertive Negotiator

An organized overview of their needs is brought to the bargaining table by assertive negotiators. They are honest and upfront when sharing needs and boundaries. They strike a balance between the urge to stand up for themselves and respecting the other person's differences and needs.

Assertive negotiators frequently adopt the stance that:

- Deals can be made
- Deals are better made when one is thoughtful and patient
- Improved results come from pursuing honesty and clarity
- Contracts must be signed

Under the assertive negotiator we have three categories: soft negotiators, hard negotiators, and principled negotiators.

Soft

These individuals prefer a gentle approach to bargaining since they view it as being too similar to competitiveness. They make offers that are not in their best interests, give in to demands made by others, avoid conflict, and keep excellent ties with other negotiators. Their aim is agreement, and they view other people as friends. They are soft on both the issue and the people, not separating the two. They abstain from will-battles and insist on consensus, proposing fixes, and readily altering their minds.

Hard

They threaten people, mistrust other people, are adamant about their position, and put pressure on others to bargain. They view people as rivals, and victory is their ultimate objective. They also look for a single solution and urge that you accept it. They are harsh on the parties involved and the issue at hand rather than separating the people from it (as with soft bargainers).

Principled

By avoiding attachment to particular ideas, people who negotiate in this way look for integrative solutions. They give more attention to the issue than to the needs, wants, and intentions of the parties concerned. They separate the individuals from the issue, investigate interests, stay away from the bottom line, and arrive at conclusions using criteria that are not dependent on the individual's desire. Instead of being swayed by influence, pressure, self-interest, or a random decision-making process, they make decisions based on objective criteria. These standards could be based on moral standards, fairness ideals, professional standards, or tradition.

Example of principled negotiation:

I could have agreed to have Mimi drop her child off at my crèche and get my daily pay. I charge $20 per day. Mimi has an important appointment and she is offering $40, but we could both clearly see that her little baby Kate has got a bad flu. I'd rather be $20 or $40 short of my money today and have Mimi take her to see a doctor instead. I'm doing this to protect other kids from getting flu. She seems at a dilemma because she badly needed to have baby Kate kept in a crèche for the day as she had no other options. So I suggest she pays a $140 so I can keep her in a separate section from other kids where I could hire an intern pediatrician to look after her.

A villain negotiator can choose to negotiate with the aggressive or assertive voice and pedal with the hard or principled style. Some experts advise negotiators to use a variety of strategies to find the best resolution to their issues; however this is frequently not the case because most people tend to tilt toward one or the other, depending on their proclivities.

Do any of the above negotiation strategies or frames of mind strike you as being familiar? If so, make sure to note it down. As you read further, you might be able to develop an assertive and successful negotiating style that yields results, however, you need to have the basic skills required.

BASIC SKILLS TO HAVE AS A NEGOTIATOR

There are a few abilities you must strive to possess if you want to enhance the results of future negotiations or if you lack confidence in your capacity to reach an effective agreement. You can be ready to maximize the value you and your counterparts leave the negotiating table with by devoting time and effort to creating them. Here is a list of the six abilities you must acquire in order to master the art of negotiating, as well as tips on how to increase your knowledge and self-assurance.

1. Interaction

It's important to communicate your goals and boundaries during negotiations in order to get the results you're hoping for. You can have civil discussions with other negotiators and work toward an amicable resolution when you have effective communication skills. Deal-making naturally involves giving and receiving, so it's critical to express your ideas clearly and pay attention to the requirements and needs of others. Without this ability, important debate points may be missed, making it impossible for all parties to come away from the negotiation satisfied.

2. Emotional intelligence

Emotions affect negotiations in both good and bad ways. While it's crucial to avoid letting them stand in the way of coming to a mutually beneficial agreement, you can still take use of them. Positive emotions, for instance, have been demonstrated to improve sentiments of trust at the negotiating table, while negative emotions, such as fear or nervousness, can be transformed into excitement.

To read the feelings of other people, one must possess a high level of emotional intelligence. This can make it easier for you to understand what they're implying rather than outright saying. Emotional intelligence can assist you in successfully managing and using emotions during a negotiation in addition to helping you comprehend what you and others are going through.

3. Planning

Any negotiation must start with a clear plan of what you want to accomplish and where your boundaries are. Without sufficient planning, you run the risk of forgetting crucial deal terms.

Think about your zone of potential agreement (ZOPA) with the other negotiating parties first. ZOPA, also known as the bargaining zone, describes the area of a negotiation where two or more sides can come to an agreement. When the conditions that both sides are willing to accept overlap, a positive negotiation zone exists. The opposite is true when neither party's terms overlap—this is known as a negative negotiating zone.

Understanding your best substitute for a negotiated agreement is then advantageous (BATNA). Your BATNA is the action you intend to take if the negotiation is unsuccessful if your conversation enters a negative bargaining zone. Knowing your BATNA in advance can ensure that you have a fallback strategy in case an agreement cannot be reached and prevent you from walking away from the table empty-handed.

4. Value creation

One of the most effective abilities you can develop for your negotiation toolkit is the ability to add value. Its significance can be best understood by using the following analogy: During negotiations, each party usually strives to get the largest "piece of the pie" possible. This inevitably means that some parties will be left with a much smaller piece because each party will be trying to maximize their slice.

Experts advise changing your focus from expanding your slice of the pie to expanding the entire pie in order to break free from this conventional notion of negotiating. The advantages are dual: Each participant can first realize more value, and talks in the future can profit from the development of rapport and trust.

5. Strategy

You require a deep understanding of negotiation strategies in addition to the capacity to add value and careful preparation. For each negotiation you take part in, you can develop a customized approach by understanding what works and what doesn't.

Think about the following actions to create a powerful bargaining strategy:

- What is your role?
- Recognize your value
- Recognize your opponent's vantage point.

- Review your own situation

You may create a precise plan of action for the negotiation table by using this approach in advance of each negotiation. You can better prepare to collaborate toward a similar objective by understanding the responsibilities of those involved, the value each party contributes, and your counterpart's advantages. Throughout the conversation, check in with yourself to make sure you're staying on the right track.

6. Reflection

Finally, you need to evaluate prior discussions and pinpoint areas for development in order to complete your negotiating skills and advance your proficiency. Reflect on what went well and what could have gone better following each negotiation, whether it was successful or not. By doing this, you'll be able to assess the strategies that were successful for you and those that weren't.

Make a list of the things you wish to work on after assessing your strengths and limitations. Consider revisiting ideas like ZOPA and BATNA, for instance, if you had problems getting your goals in sync with those of your partner. Or, if you frequently feel unsatisfied after negotiations, you can benefit from discovering new ways to add value.

In developing your negotiating skills, no matter your abilities and limitations, practicing regularly will help you improve. You'll be more equipped for future transactions the more talks you engage in.

Find opportunities to negotiate as a practical experience which can sharpen your consciousness on the thoughts and behaviour patterns of other people during negotiations. Not shying away from tough negotiations can help you gain insight into how others are prepared to handle challenging conversations, and when you lose, bag the experience as it would better prepare you to deal with other opportunities along the line and when you do win, you can note down the strategies that led to those successful negotiations.

MEET THE VILLAIN

A compelling antagonist is necessary for every life story to be genuinely remarkable. Sometimes the antagonist is so captivating that the hero is overshadowed. That isn't always a terrible thing, both in fiction and reality. Many times we fall in love with our villains because of the enthralling character they possess. Ever been to a Halloween party? All that mattered was that people were masked in power, whether it was a protagonist or antagonist kind of power doesn't really matter, but the question is, who commands more fear and admiration?

So how can you create a villain in yourself that if you were on screen, you would inspire a million Halloween costumes? Firstly, you need to recognize the traits that are shared by some of the most admired villains and emulate them:

1. Powerful

Great villains are extremely powerful. To put it another way, they have a talent for bending reality to their will. This frequently takes the shape of magical abilities in fantasy literature. Perhaps a powerful sorcerer or a fallen Jedi Knight is the villain. However, sometimes the villain's strength comes from his wealth. He might be incredibly powerful and wealthy. Or, he might be in control of a well-trained army.

However, sometimes the villain's strength is less clear. The femme fatale, a lady who utilizes her charm to manipulate those around her, is a well-known literary figure. Some villains are far more deadly than heroes because they have strong intelligence and cunning.

2. Intelligent

Intelligent villains are successful. This does not imply that they are inherently intelligent. Instead, it implies that people refrain from making poor choices.

Sometimes inexperienced people make the mistake of assuming villains are just like the types often depicted in movies, who are so enamored with their own desire that they act foolishly. Such a person is not a compelling antagonist, however they might make for amusing caricatures. A truly brilliant villain always thinks two steps ahead of the hero and weighs all of his options carefully.

This does not imply that they are impervious to error. Otherwise, they would be impossible to defeat. However, they almost never choose the obvious ones. Great villains are at the top of their game, which makes them a true challenge for the hero.

3. Immoral

Real villains lack morality. They are villains because of this. It's not that they don't understand what is good and wrong. On the other hand, villains frequently follow a moral code. But in order to achieve their objectives, they are prepared to go outside accepted moral standards.
Grindelwald from the Harry Potter series is a good example. He is aware that he has transgressed every standard of decency, but he claims that his activities are "for the greater good," which excuses them. He believes that maintaining the ideal social order is so crucial that it requires torturous actions.

A lot of excellent villains have this trait. They no longer

regard themselves as being subject to the accepted norms of moral behavior because they have such a strong belief in the righteousness of their own cause.

4. Wounded

Usually, memorable villains are broken people. This can sometimes take the form of physical injuries or deformities, as shown in the scarred face of the Joker or the amputated limbs of Darth Vader. The most significant wounds, however, are most frequently psychological or emotional.

This illustrates the important lesson that no one is born a monster. Instead, the harm and cruelty committed upon people turns them into monsters. An innocent child must have experienced something to change him into a murderous adult. Even if the character's tragic past isn't fully developed in the novel, it is frequently alluded to.

Additionally, having a wounded villain keeps the bad guy from turning into a caricature. It's a fantasy cliché to have villains that are consumed by a hunger for power. It becomes convincing if the character has a justification for their lust.

5. Determined

The distinction between the big villains and the lesser baddies is made by this. A genuinely formidable villain is driven by an unquenchable desire to succeed. Never in a million years will he give up (unless he is somehow redeemed, which will be the subject of a future article).

The Dark Lord himself, Sauron of Mordor, is perhaps the most obvious example. Even the loss of his physical body is simply a setback for him because of how determined he is to rule Middle Earth. When a great evil sets his sights on anything, nothing less than annihilation will stand in his way. This heightens the danger of the hero's defiance.

6. Unpredictable: this trait can put the other party off balance, becloud their thoughts, and make them confused and unable to tell the next move of a true villain.

7. Calculative: the villain has a steadily processing mind; they premeditate and weigh the moves of their opponent and the effect of theirs on their opponent even before they find themselves in that phase of dealing, their thinking ahead helps them get what they want from people.

8. Fearless: braveness and confidence is a major trait of a villain, they aren't afraid of dealing with new people from all walks of life. When your opponent finds you dauntless, you are more likely to command respect than if you were spineless.

9. Dominant: the dominant personality is the villain exhibits when he leads himself and others into action, this trait comes with a sense of pride and an overarching motivation, this is one of the elements of their power tussle and influence over their opponent.

10. Enigmatic: this personality trait enshrouds a villain behind his words and smiles, making him mysterious to others.

11. Ambitious: this trait pushes the villain to set goals and determine to achieve them. The ambitious villain never backs down; they aim higher and have strong desire to get ahead of even the best of their

peers. They strive to eliminate anything in the way of their ambitions.

12. Charming: the villain is often likeable, they activate the friendly, pleasant attitude in order to win people's hearts – a very deliberate act; it is this likeability that he uses to have his way with counterparts who have fallen for his charms.

These traits put together make for a strong villain; some of us have one or more of these traits inside of us. This list, however, is not meant to be comprehensive. There are probably several qualities that I have overlooked in order to retain appropriate context. Now I leave the rest up to you. What qualities do you consider to be necessary for a great villain, look within you, which among all do you possess?

THE TACTICS OF MIND GAMES

Playing mind games, also known as power games or head games, involves an effort to psychologically outwit another person. Passive-aggressive tactics are sometimes used to intentionally demoralize or disempower the thinking subject, giving the aggressor the appearance of superiority. Additionally, it defines the hidden games people play while engaging in transactions they are not completely aware of, which transactional analysis views as a key component of social life worldwide.

Mind tricks can be employed in close relationships to challenge one partner's confidence in the veracity of their own views. Personal experience may be suppressed and erased from memory, and such manipulative mind games may also deny the victim's reality, undermine their reputation, and minimize their partner's worries. Equal opportunity exists for such verbal coercion from both sexes and may be used unintentionally in order to sustain one's own self-deception.

In the context of the pursuit of prestige, mind games frequently occur in the workplace, in sports, and in romantic relationships. It might be difficult to distinguish between office mind games and over-directing, healthy competition and sabotage, and strong management. The cautious salesperson will be mentally and emotionally ready to deal with a variety of difficult mind tricks and jabs during their workday. The serious sportsperson will also be ready to deal with a range of gambits and head games from their competitors, trying to balance competitive psychology and paranoia.

Before approaching the negotiating table, there are a few psychological phenomena you should be aware of and, if you're good enough, you might be able to exploit them to your advantage.

Illustrations of mind games used in negotiations:

- The first and most well-known mind trick is "anchoring," which is when a negotiator starts a distributive conversation with a suggestion that places the conversation close to his or her aim. The choice of the initial value is not very fascinating in and of itself, but what is fascinating is how frequently the negotiator on the opposing side of the transaction will alter his or her beginning position to approach that value. Therefore, be careful not to fall for this ploy by keeping to the first offer you would have made while you're at the negotiating table and your opponent offers their first number before you've given your own. However, you might benefit from this by making the first offer in the negotiation.

- *'Supplies Limited! Call Now!'*
The apparent availability of the subject of the negotiation is the focus of the "availability bias," another form of judgment bias. It should come as no surprise that the economist in you will tell you that something is more valuable if you believe it to be uncommon than if it is widely available.

- "Everyone's Doing It"

  You'll frequently hear negotiators explain why their offer

is fair after it has been put on the table. They are aiming to capitalize on the well-known "framing" prejudice by doing this. According to studies, people frequently rely their decisions on some kind of outside standard, such as the accepted "status quo" or custom. In light of this, bringing up the fact that "everyone is doing it" may not be such a straw man argument after all.

- Present a Red Herring to them

    Giving someone a second option that highlights the advantages of the one you want them to choose is another strategy for influencing their decision. As an illustration, most people would select the cash if given the option between $6 and a quality pen. However, customers would choose the better pen over the $6 alternative far more often if you also offered a third option of a lower-quality pen. So, if you're giving various packages, think about including one that you don't think they'll choose but is more in line with the option you'd like they choose.

STRATEGIES AND TACTICS OF A VILLAIN NEGOTIATOR

For years, I've learnt through hands-on experience that no doesn't always mean "NO" sometimes it can actually imply "know". It's possible that the person you're chatting with lacks the knowledge or authorization to respond to your query.

For instance, it's always preferable to speak with a supervisor who has the authority to say yes when phoning a financial services organization about a credit card situation or anything else. According to Sir Winston Churchill: "Never accept defeat; never take no for an answer." This is the mind of a villain negotiator. It is often in such shameless persistence that you breakthrough, it is the reason why instead of accepting the possibility of losing in a negotiation just yet, you weave out strategies and tactics to ensure that the odds are on your side for the winning. Having understood fully the traits of villains as mentioned above and the power of mind games, we can now pull together the strategies that often lead to a win with which they negotiate.

Auction:

People desire things more when they are aware that they could miss out on them so villains create FOMO (fear of missing out) through auctions, either outright or using its undertones. The goal of the bidding procedure is to foster competition. Put parties in opposition to one another when they both desire the same thing. They want the item that is being bid on, but they also want to win for the sake of winning. Taking advantage of a person's competitiveness can raise the cost; this is a fact villains are familiar with.

Example:

I auction things to stimulate fear of missing out and close deals quicker. I run my digital assets trading group where I give daily trade signals and I determine the number of members I want to have, but I tell potential customers there's only five slots left and people are bidding to pay $1000 per slot. As soon as my potential clients got this message I got a hike in membership requests – people were placing bids around $1000 to get membership for something that was initially worth $500. I had doubled my profit on membership fees by auctioning it to stimulate FOMO and close deals quicker.

Brinkmanship:

A negotiating partner is forced to accept the terms the other party is pursuing aggressively or leave the table. Brinkmanship is a form of "hard nut" negotiating in which one party drives the other to the "brink" or limit of what that party will accept. Successful brinkmanship persuades the opposing party that there is no other option than to accept the offer and that the suggested deal is the only one that can be reached.

Example:

If you walk out of this car repair shop the next car repair services with specialization in Mercedes Benz is 10km away. Why go through that stress or burn your fuel to get there while we can do a good job? Bear in mind that the car repair shops close-by are smaller and may not properly diagnose your Mercedes faults as they repair general brands. Besides, they might charge more due to the big brand factor, think about that.

Bogey:

The bogeyman strategy is used by negotiators to make a minor or unimportant problem seem crucial. The issue can then be exchanged for a significant concession that actually matters later in the negotiation. An example is that of the journalist who found a dead mouse in his hotel suite bathroom and struck a bargain with the hotel manager. Here's another instance below.

Example:

Customer: *Is that a scratch on the Adidas shoe? I wouldn't pay that amount, a 5% off would be just perfect. That scratch is a spoiler! Or perhaps...I can pick the Nike in exchange.*

Sales officer: *That Nike costs more than the Adidas.*

Customer: *I would like to have the Nike in place of the Adidas or a 5% discount on the Adidas, the ball is in your court.*

Contacting a higher power:

One party makes the outcome of future negotiations contingent on the choice of a decision maker who is not physically present at the negotiation table in an effort to water down too much concession, deescalate, or break a deadlock. It gives them time to come through the most favourable angles to them and create the idea of a higher power which they cannot go against.

Example:

Ok, I'll check with my boss if that price is okay.

The man at the top is very rigid with his money, he doesn't play unfair so we cannot close the deal at that price.

Chicken:

During negotiation, extreme measures are frequently proposed in the form of bluffs, in order to coerce the other party into surrendering and giving in to their demands. When parties are unwilling to give in and carry out the drastic measure, this strategy can be disastrous.

Example:

I don't really need generators, I just wanted to acquire an alternative power source, and by the way just to let you know, I'm aware you've reached out to my organization, I'm currently going to campaign to my colleagues to hold on purchasing generators and use solar panels because they are cost-effective. If you can make it cheaper then I'll purchase one and drop my campaign plans so that my colleagues can patronize you as well.

Defense in Depth:

To allow for more compromises each time the agreement passes through a different level of authority, several levels of decision-making authority are used. To put it another way, every time the offer is presented to a decision-maker, that person requests the addition of another concession to seal the deal.

Example:

I know you've spent quite a lot on consultation fees but you have to bargain and settle with the higher authorities first before we can grant you the authority to carry on with the project. It doesn't all end on this table; if you are able to cross higher hurdles then we can seal the deal.

Deadlines:

Set a deadline for the other party to decide, forcing them to do so. This approach applies pressure to the other party over time. Given deadlines may be real or made up.

Example:

Agent: We got insider information that our boss is giving the apartment out for rent to a best friend in 3 days' time if it remains vacant till then. We want you not to miss out on this offer, you have at most two days to think about it and reach out to us ASAP.

Flinch:

A suggestion is met with a significant negative physical reaction when someone flinches. Flinching frequently manifests as gasping for air or a visibly surprised or shocked countenance. Both consciously and involuntarily, people can flinch. By flinching, you are trying to get the other party to reduce their standards by signaling to them that you find the offer or proposition ludicrous. Hearing someone say, "I'm astonished," is less credible than seeing a physical response.

Example:

Customer: how much is this dress?

Sales person: it costs only $600

Customer: drops jaw and clasps hands on cheek "that is friggin' expensive!

Sales person: smiles uneasily and looks again at the dress considering that it might be truly overpriced.

Forgiveness Math:

According to computer simulated studies, the best course of action is to make peace with your adversary or give them the chance to work with you to find a solution that benefits both parties. Negotiators must safeguard their own interests and be ready for lack of collaboration because, of course, the worst negotiators are those who do not understand their own self-interest.

Example:

Although we have been unfriendly competitors in the pig farming business, we need to fight the recent scourge together, mostly, we ought to investigate our suspects who have formulated and spread this disease so we can collectively sue them for our losses.

Generous Tit for Tat:

So many negotiators try to utilize a macho and deceitful style that mirrors the world's abuse of power. They strut around and act smart, but in reality they have never learned or practiced effective negotiation techniques. This act is an example of some of the worst and most repulsive leadership in the world. Real-world study demonstrates the advantages of a skilled and knowledgeable collaborative style.

Example:

Mayor of Chicago in February 2011, Rahm Emanuel, annulled a promised pay raise for school teachers and lobbied the Illinois state legislature to place a limit on the issues the Chicago Teachers Union (CTU) could bargain and strike over. Although this worked temporarily, failed contract negotiations between the CTU and the City of Chicago still resulted in a 10-day teachers' strike in the middle of 2012, and this also resulted in a settlement that gave gains for both parties, including an extension of the school day and yearly teacher raises.

Good vs. Evil:

In the good guy/bad guy strategy (also known as good cop/bad cop or black hat/white hat), tasks that are both pleasant and unpleasant are frequently split between two negotiators on the same side of the bargaining table, or unpleasant tasks or decisions are given to a (actual or fictitious) outsider. The good man endorses signing the contract and highlights successful areas of the negotiations (mutual interests). The wicked man calls out negative characteristics (opposing interests). The separation of the two roles enables the individual negotiators to behave consistently and with greater credibility. The good guy can gain the other side's trust by promoting the pact.

Example:

"I'm donating a good portion of the profit I make to charity," says Mike, a sly negotiator who was about closing a deal with his client, an NGO representative. The NGO ended up paying more cash because Mike had fronted the "charity" cause to prevent them from bargaining for a much lower price, because apparently, shortening his profits would mean shortening the amount of aid that goes to the charity home. That would ultimately make his counterpart negotiator the insensitive guy with little to no consideration of the needy and he, the good guy, regardless of what amount truly went to charity.

Highball/Low-ball or Ambit claim:

Depending on whether they are buying or selling, sellers or buyers will make an unrealistically high or low initial offer. A further benefit is that the party making the extreme demand appears more flexible when they make concessions toward a more reasonable outcome. The theory is that the extreme offer forces the other party to reevaluate their own opening offer and move close to the resistance point (as far as you are willing to go to reach an agreement). This strategy has the risk of making the other side believe that it is pointless to negotiate.

Example:

Mr Williams needs a minimum of 50 labourers and he decides to negotiate for a deal at a workforce company.

"I'm paying $10,000 for 100 laborers in my construction site." Mr Williams negotiates with the agent.

"But the adequate pay is $400 per labourer," Replied the agent "This means that $10,000 can only pay for 25 labourers at this period!"

Williams tugs at his beards "25 laborers is extremely poor from the 100 men I require. If I take my $10,000 dollars to some other company, I could close a better deal"

Agent says "You drive a hard bargain Mr. Williams…since you stand at 100 and I stand at 25, if you came down by 50% and I went up by 100%, since I have the smaller figure, we could have a good meeting point. I can make it a total of 50 laborers. I'm being quite generous."

Williams says "good deal."

The nibble:

Nibbling, sometimes referred to as the salami tactic or the quivering quill, is the demand for proportionately little concessions that have not been previously negotiated immediately before the deal is sealed. By saying, "Just one more thing," this tactic takes advantage of the other person's desire to close.

Example:

The workforce agent, aware that Mr. Williams has saved some money from the bargain and is burning with a hasty desire to seal the deal, chips in "just one more thing"

"What could that be?" Mr Williams asked with brows pulled together. The agent's request would definitely be to his own advantage because the more the labourer agreed upon, the higher the value of his "additional request".

He then replies "The laborers lunch and conveyance is on you, I mean, you will be too busy to be making such arrangements and you do not want workers leaving the site in hunt for food in the middle of their job. That's time wasting."

"I didn't think about that." Mr Williams said plainly.

"I'll do the arrangements; I'll have $35 per laborer lunch pack and two hired buses with everything they'll need for their welfare, to convey them, and that will be settled. In total that's just an extra $ 2500 and we're good."

Mr. Williams, at this point, knows that he has already struck a good enough bargain with the initial negotiation and is eager to close the deal and get started so he agrees to the "little necessary additions."

Snow job:

By providing the opposing party with so much information, negotiators make it impossible for them to distinguish between what information is crucial and what is a distraction. In order to disguise a straightforward response to a query posed by a non-expert, negotiators may use utilize jargon or specialized terminology. This is very common, especially with technical repairs.

Example:

Linda: *I said to my car mechanic, that my car is making a weird noise, it sounds gulug, gulug, gulug; I think there might be a tiny fault. He took a few minutes to check my car and discovered a million things I needed to fix or replace. As he spoke, I stood there staring at him like he was talking complete gobbledydook! Could he be doing this because I'm a woman, and I'm clueless about car garage jargons? Just what the heck is he saying?*

Mechanic: *According to diagnostics check, your big end has gone, the bushes were on the way out, the brakes...spongy, there's sign of mayonnaise under the old cap, and the side needs a bondo.*

I knew that the mechanic might have bamboozled me and grabbed a few more bucks out of my purse but then, what the heck else could I have done? I was dizzy with confusion at those terminologies!

Mirroring:

The outcome of a negotiation is more likely to be favorable when participants get along well. A negotiator may imitate or duplicate the opponent's behavior and repeat what they say in order to build rapport and establish trust. When someone mirrors, they recite the main points of another person's recent speech or imitate a specific facial expression. It signals that the other party's opinion or statement has been taken into consideration during the negotiating process. Mirroring can support connection building and trust-building.

Example:

To show the hostage taker that I was all ears, I could feel his plight and I understand every word coming out of his mouth, I reiterated all he said and mimicked his demeanor and countenances. He is trying to hurry everyone involved into giving him the money he's requesting. Our movements and body language are becoming rapid too, as though yielding to his hurrying gestures and working with his desired timing. He's seemingly convinced we are quickly going to gather the money he asks.

We want him to trust us as though we are collaborating but we intend to stall him with a few distractions till the police find him.

"The bank is closed, the cash app is experiencing bad network, what other means of payment can you accept? Do I use the ATM and bring the cash in a duffle bag?" I say to him, speaking as fast as I could.

Anchoring:

Establishing a reference point first in order to lead the other party closer to your offered price is known as "anchoring." It is frequently brought up at the outset of a negotiation in an effort to sway the conversation moving forward. The reverse is also true when purchasing something. Here, we're supposed to reduce or increase the expectations of the other parties. You should draw attention to the fact that they are anchoring and demand that they lower the price to a reasonable level in order to combat anchoring.

Example:

I wish to sell a car for $50,000. Now a customer enters and declares they wish to purchase a car. I declare that the car would be sold for $65,000. Since I made the offer first, I have a little vantage point. The other person will need to up his counter offer to draw closer to mine till we agree. The customer would probably counteroffer for $50,000 to $55,000.

Silence:

This is a powerful negotiation tool; it is enigmatic and makes a negotiator unpredictable. The villain negotiator knows how and when to use this tool as it is tremendously unsettling and cause an adversary to ramble in fear and confusion.

As an employer, when my new staff summoned the courage to ask for a raise, which I knew was due already, I opened the floor for him to suggest an offer and as soon as he asked for a 10% of his total pay I went into silence, sitting across the table from him I could feel the heat from his body as the silence prolonged. He sweated and fidgeted, he felt as though his request was considered outrageous, yet he gave me my time to think, brood, consider, seethe – whatever the silence was for. He wondered if he had put his entire position at stake. When I finally spoke, i pinned it down to 5%, with his reaction he seemed relieved and I think he was glad that the torment of my long silence had come to an end too. It was a deal.

EMOTIONS AND BODY LANGUAGE DURING NEGOTIATION

Ever wondered why people regard physical negotiation as the most effective type? This is because that's the only way emotions and body language of the other party can be assessed. Although we are in a digital world but instead of relying on the phone or the Internet always, try as much as you can to make physical negotiations. Despite how convenient electronic media may be, they lack the visual indications that body language provides in negotiations to help people connect and transmit important information. Those who negotiate at a distance have difficulty effectively reading each other's tones and developing rapport since they lack access to gestures and facial expressions.

According to psychologists and language experts, nonverbal cues and body language have a bigger influence on a conversation than the words you say. Studies have proven that body language is a more reliable indicator of someone's genuine views and intentions than their tone of voice or words. More than 55% of communications are communicated by nonverbal clues like gestures and posture. According to studies, people are 80% more likely to remember information that is presented to them visually and verbally.

The point we are driving at is that one's emotions and body

language plays a big role during negotiation because they help to assess how each other feels about each conversation holding up the entire bargain, in fact, body language can most times tell you outrightly if it's already a done deal or not.

Body languages in negotiation and what they imply:

- A nervous laugh: this is usually one that doesn't fit the circumstance. This can indicate anxiety or discomfort. When this occurs, it may be wise to ask follow-up questions to elicit the other person's genuine emotions.
- Positive words but negative body language: When asked if they are annoyed, a negotiation partner may clench their fist and snap back, "What makes you believe anything is bothering me?"
- Clasped hands lifted in the air: Even when smiling, the person raises their hands in this manner to express dissatisfaction. This is a clue that the person performing it might be suppressing a bad attitude.
- Inability to maintain eye contact: this can imply the party is not being honest or is hiding something
- demonstrating receptivity

    Partners in a negotiation may be more open to one other's thoughts and messages depending on how their bodies are positioned in relation to one another:

    i. Face and eyes: Negotiators who are receptive smile and make lots of eye contact. Conversely, non-receptive negotiators hardly ever initiate eye contact. They can have their head slightly tilted away from the speaker, their eyes squinted, and their jaw clinched.

    ii. Arms and hands: Negotiators should spread their arms wide and place their hands open on the table or relaxed on their laps to display receptivity. When hands are clasped, crossed, placed in front of the lips, or rubbed behind the back, negotiators exhibit low receptivity.

iii. Legs and feet: Receptive negotiators sit with their legs crossed or slightly in front of one another. They stand with their weight equally distributed, hands on hips, and bodies tilted toward the speaker. Legs crossed and erect, non-receptive negotiators face away from the speaker.

iv. Torso: Receptive negotiators lean forward in their chairs, unbuttoning their sport coats as they do so. Negotiators who are not open to compromise might recline in their chairs and keep their suit coats buttoned.

Here's how to use the right non-verbal cues and body language during negotiations

1. Arrive on time

A prospective client, potential boss, or business rival will form their opinion of you even before you enter the room or speak a word. In two ways, being late hurts the bargaining process: The opposing party will become irritated and less likely to want to achieve an agreement since, in the first place, it is seen as disrespectful (or even offensive) and suggests incompetence and lack of integrity on the side of the latecomer.

Second, the stress that you'll undoubtedly feel as a result of being late will derail the composed, concentrated, and confident attitude that you'll need to conjure if you want to succeed in the negotiation itself. So arrive on time and give yourself a chance.

2. The handshake

A simple handshake is sufficient otherwise a solid handshake would be more indicative of eagerness and friendliness. The fact that you shake hands at all is essentially the only thing that matters about your handshake and there is no emphasis on how perfect or strong or stylish it is. A handshake, improves cooperative behaviors that lead to deal making, helps individuals feel at ease, and encourages honesty.

3. Maintain friendly eye contact

According to William Shakespeare, "the eyes are the windows of the soul" while directing his words at businesspeople, politicians, and poker players. Eye contact is one of the most effective ways to communicate since it demonstrates openness, sincerity, and trust between two individuals.

In a negotiation, avoiding eye contact prevents a positive rapport from growing. It conveys the impression that you are being evasive or dishonest, which both make bargaining exceedingly challenging. However, because eye contact has such a strong impact, using it excessively can be frightening and perceived as aggressive or intimidating. Although you should maintain fairly constant eye contact, bear in mind that it's normal to avert your gaze while considering or processing anything.

4. Pay attention to your facial expressions.

It's not necessary to be a business magnate to be aware of the frequently undesirable effects your unintended facial expressions can have on a conversation's conclusion. Anyone who has ever been in a relationship has probably felt the utter aggravation that comes from having a conversation interrupted by their spouse asking, "What does that look mean?!"

Whether you like it or not, your facial expressions will be scrutinized in a negotiation situation, so make sure they support the good verbal indications you're offering. Be careful not to worry-wrinkle your forehead, and whenever you can, smile and nod your head in agreement. Keep your eyes level and your chin up to project positivity. Keep in mind that the other person will be watching to see if your bodily movements and words are consistent.

5. Proxemics: Maintain personal space

The study of personal space, sometimes known as "Proxemics," is concerned with the separation of individuals during social interactions. Have you ever experienced extreme pressure or discomfort as a result of someone standing a bit too closely while conversing with you? To the extent that you lost interest in the talk and began to shuffle your feet while want them to move farther away?

As you may expect, a scenario like this absolutely shatters the negotiation process. It's critical that both parties feel respected in their personal space and aren't being physically intimidated. A good rule of thumb is to sit or stand four feet apart and observe the other person to see how comfortable they are. Villain negotiators can counter this tactical advantage by arranging allies to surround the individual.

6. Keep your limbs relaxed and open.

During a negotiation, your body should convey the same strength, confidence, and composure that you wish to convey with your words. It will be obvious that you are stressed, rather than being thoughtful, if you are frequently tapping your fingers or feet, entwining your hands, or crossing and uncrossing your legs. Keep your hands to expressing yourself and avoid fidgeting at the expense of your legs.

Communication of interpersonal attitudes and feelings through nonverbal channels is 12.5 times more effective than communication through verbal channels. Similar to this, any degree of crossed limbs or hands will be perceived as negative and closed off, which will hinder your ability to inspire trust in any discussion. Nobody wants to converse with someone who appears to have made up their mind! As a result, uncross your arms and legs and keep some space between your hands to give the impression that you are open-minded and willing to hear the opinions of others.

7. Hands-down

Speaking of hands, they can add a lot to your conversation because they are very expressive. The usual rule of thumb is to keep your hands away from your face while bargaining. Being worried is the last thing you want to come across as, and rubbing one's face or head is typically considered as a symptom of anxiousness.

Similarly, covering your mouth or eyes with your hands suggests that you might be lying or trying to hide. Keep your hands as open, unclenched, and far from your face as possible to project an air of assurance and sincerity.

8. Be quiet and slow down

Everyone wants to believe that their opinions have been heard, appreciated, and taken into account before a countermove is made, regardless of the circumstance. Nevertheless, the tension of the negotiation can cause you to become jumpy and overexcited, rushing your words or even talking over the other person out of excitement and the desire to convey your point. When the other person finishes speaking, stop briefly to show that you are considering what they have said. Then, respond slowly and calmly. This communicates respect but also confidence in your leadership.

Only 20% of information shown to people visually and 10% of information presented to them audibly is remembered by individuals. However, a person retains 80% of the information that is conveyed to them verbally and visually, implying that using body language is just as significant as speaking.

Additionally, don't be afraid to be silent for a brief period of time in order to play on the other person's fears. You may be surprised by the results.

"Never forget the power of silence, that massively disconcerting pause which goes on and on and may at last induce an opponent to babble and backtrack nervously."

-Lance Murrow

Effects of emotions during negotiation

Although their impact has only recently been researched, emotions play a significant role in the negotiation process. Emotions may influence negotiations in a favorable or unfavorable way. The choice of whether or not to settle during negotiations is influenced by emotional variables. Negative feelings can lead to passionate, even illogical behavior, which can intensify disagreements and lead to a breakdown in talks, but they can also be helpful in getting concessions. Positive feelings, on the other hand, can be useful in obtaining concessions since they frequently make it easier to come to a consensus and to maximize shared benefits. Positive and negative discrete emotions may manifest differently across cultural boundaries and can be purposefully exhibited to affect task and relationship results.

Cause effect

Dispositions influence different aspects of negotiation, including which techniques to use, which strategies are actually chosen, how the other party and their intentions are perceived, their readiness to come to a compromise, and the eventual outcomes of the negotiation. The negotiation parties' positive affectivity (PA) and negative affectivity (NA) might produce drastically diverse results.

Positive affect

People in a good mood are more confident and more likely to prepare to utilize a cooperative tactic even before the negotiation process begins. Negotiators who are in a good mood during the negotiation tend to enjoy the encounter more, behave less combatively, employ less aggressive techniques, and use more cooperative strategies. This in turn improves the potential to uncover integrative gains and raises the possibility that parties will achieve their instrumental aims. In fact, when compared to negotiators with negative or natural affectivity, those with positive affectivity were able to negotiate more agreements and were more likely to uphold them. Better decision-making processes, such as flexible thinking, inventive problem-solving, respect for others' perspectives, willingness to take chances, and stronger confidence, are responsible for these favorable outcomes. Positive post-negotiation reaction also produces advantageous side effects. It influences a person's desire for future contacts and raises satisfaction with the attained result. By facilitating the mutual relationship and bringing commitment, the PA sparked by achieving an agreement prepares the ground for forthcoming interactions.

Additionally, PA has disadvantages since it alters how people perceive their own performance, making it appear better than it truly is. Therefore, studies that ask participants to self-report their success may be skewed.

Negative affect

Negative affect has a negative impact on many phases of the negotiation process. While several unpleasant emotions have been linked to poor negotiation results, rage has received the most attention. Even before the discussion begins, angry parties make plans to adopt more aggressive techniques and to cooperate less – reduced joint results are associated with these competitive behaviors.

The effects of anger during negotiations include a decline in trust, impaired judgment, a reduction in attention span, and a shift in the parties' primary objectives from achieving an agreement to exacting revenge on the other party. Angry negotiators produce smaller joint profits because they are less attentive to and accurate at assessing their adversaries' interests.

Additionally, anger increases the possibility that negotiators will reject lucrative offers because it causes them to become more self-centered in their choices. Make sure they are in your favor because opponents who become extremely upset (or cry, or otherwise lose control) are more prone to make mistakes. Angry negotiators fail to reach agreements which diminish the potential for joint gains and do not increase personal gains.

Also, negative emotions cause people to accept settlements that have a negative utility function rather than a positive utility function. However, expressing one's negative emotions during a negotiation can occasionally be advantageous. For example, expressing one's justifiable anger can be a powerful method to communicate one's dedication, sincerity, and requirements.

Additionally, while NA lowers gains in integrative tasks, it outperforms PA in distributive tasks (such as zero-sum). Seidner discovered evidence for the presence of a negative affect arousal mechanism in his research on negative affect arousal and white noise by making observations about the devaluation of speakers from other ethnic backgrounds. Submerged animosity toward a particular ethnic or gender group may also have a negative impact on negotiations.

Emotion effect

This theory states that emotions only influence negotiations when one is high and the other is low. The affect is recognized when both ability and motivation are low, and when both are high, the emotion is recognized but is disregarded as unimportant to judgment. This model would suggest, for instance, that the favorable impacts PA has on negotiations (as previously demonstrated) only appear when either motivation or ability are low.

Impact of a partner's emotions

The majority of research on emotion in negotiations focuses on how the negotiator's emotions affect the process. The other person's feelings, however, might be just as significant because it is known that group emotions have an impact on both group and individual processes. For an emotion to have an impact on negotiations, the opposing party must be trusted, and visibility strengthens the effect. Emotions play a role in the negotiation process by expressing one's feelings and thoughts, which might stop the other party from acting destructively and suggest the next course of action: While NA emphasizes the necessity for behavioral or mental alterations, PA suggests to continue in the same manner.

Mimetic/reciprocal or complimentary impacts on the emotions and actions of the negotiator can result from the partner's emotions. For instance, melancholy or disappointment could increase cooperation and compassion. The majority of participants in a research by Butt et al. (2005) simulating real multi-phase negotiations responded to the partner's emotions in a reciprocal rather than complementing way. Various emotions were discovered to have different impacts on the thoughts and strategies employed by the opponent:

Anger: In a zero-sum negotiation, anger made the opponents' demands lower and their concessions greater, but it also made them less favorable toward the negotiation. It prompted the opponent to act in both a dominant and submissive manner.

Pride: pride made the partner use more integrative and compromising techniques.

Guilt or regret: When the negotiator displayed guilt or regret, the opponent had a better view of him but also raised their demands. Personal guilt, on the other hand, was linked to greater pleasure with one's accomplishments.

Worry or disappointment: Though they made the opponent feel horrible, worry or disappointment actually reduced their demands.

Managing emotions during negotiations

- Make emotions explicit and validate them – By being more proactive in talking about one's sentiments, a negotiation can concentrate on the issue at hand rather than any repressed emotions. It's crucial to give both parties a chance to express their feelings.

- Allow time to vent - It's probable that one party will become irate or upset throughout the course of the negotiation. Allowing the person to express their sentiments is preferable to trying to avoid doing so. Without giving the substance itself too much feedback, simply sitting and listening can be enough to make someone feel better. Negotiations could be simpler once the complaints have been expressed.

- Symbolic actions - Take into account that an apology or any other straightforward gesture could be one of the most efficient and affordable ways to diffuse any tense feelings between the parties.

- Empathy - Your emotions will heavily influence what you say in every negotiation you engage in. Due to our tendency to project our own presumptions, we frequently overreact and misinterpret what the other party says. It's critical to turn your attention to the other side, be totally present with them, and listen to them without passing judgment in order to avoid misunderstandings and foster a collaborative environment. Only then will we be in a position to react correctly. We frequently act in our own best interests because we prioritize our own requirements and anxieties. However, when we do this, we forget about the other party, who is always the most crucial element in every discussion. You need to put yourself aside and concentrate solely on the other party, their emotions, their interests, and their concerns if you want to maximize your chances of coming to a mutually beneficial agreement. Only then will you be able to give them what they need rather than what you want. Barriers to communication dissolve when the other side feels heard and recognized, and a consensus is far more likely to be reached.

RESPONDING TO THREATS DURING NEGOTIATIONS

Take a step back and identify the issue when someone in a negotiation issues a threat or an ultimatum. Think about how you would react in a negotiation to the following threats and demands:

"You won't ever work in this industry again if you try to back out."

"If you don't comply with our demands, we'll see you in court."

"That is our last proposal. Take it or leave it."

Should you respond to such a stern discussion with a retaliatory threat?

Most likely not. Counter-threats will lead you farther off course because they inflame the tense atmosphere of a discussion. Instead, ask for a break as soon as you hear a threat (or as soon as you issue one yourself). Say something along the lines of, "It has been a long meeting. When we're feeling rested, why don't we reconvene? Rearranging the meeting will give both parties a chance to calm down and weigh their alternatives.

Analyze the threat when you're feeling more at ease, possibly with the help of a reliable friend or advisor who can give you a reality check.

Here are things to consider in such a situation:

1. Is she likely to carry on with her threat?

Sometimes during negotiations, threats are made that the negotiators later regret. You might decide to help the person preserve face by ignoring the threat if it is obvious that they have no intention of following through on their threat and if they appear repentant or embarrassed about it.

The same is true when a rival openly threatens you—the threat may not even be directed at you. She can be attempting to maintain her good reputation with people inside or outside the negotiation.

Be careful that she might genuinely be hoping that you won't take the threat seriously in these situations.

That seemed to be the case when, in the midst of the October 1962 Cuban Missile Crisis, Soviet Premier Nikita Khrushchev made a strident public demand to President John F. Kennedy. After Kennedy learned that the Soviet Union was constructing a missile site in Cuba, there was a tense standoff between the two nuclear superpowers.

Khrushchev secretly made an offer to demolish the installations in exchange for Kennedy's vow not to invade Cuba. However, the Soviets made a formal request for the United States to evacuate its own missile systems from Turkey the following day.

Kennedy chose to accept the gentler private message rather than comply with this demand, which was a decision that helped to defuse the situation and his brother Robert's counsel.

2. Threats shouldn't always be disregarded.

You need to diffuse the issue if you believe a disgruntled supplier would actually carry out his threat to damage your reputation.

Even if a threat seems to be a bluff, the other side may be trying to get your attention by expressing a very serious desire to be understood.

Get to the heart of the topic by using active listening techniques, "Listen Up!"

Inquiry may reveal misunderstandings and enable you to work together to "alter the game" and lead conversations in a more cooperative direction by pressing the other side to explain the motivation behind the threat.

Acknowledging the feelings concealed in the other person's message—what he is not saying—is the third and most challenging step of attentive listening.

You can say to the irate customer, "I'm detecting a lot of dissatisfaction on your behalf." Before we try to move forward, I'd like to know more about your feelings."

Talking about the feelings that underlie threats might help to defuse conflict and reestablish your common ground.

3. What did I do to trigger the threat?

If you actively listen, you might notice that your counterpart's threat is being motivated by valid grievances and concerns. By raising these issues, you both strengthen your own argument and demonstrate to the opposing side your concern for and understanding of her viewpoint. Of course, promising to make things right when you've harmed someone is insufficient. You'll need to act quickly to follow through.

After failing to strike a deal to pay media behemoth Viacom to host Viacom content on Google's YouTube video-sharing subsidiary, Internet corporation Google appeared to learn that lesson. In contravention of copyright laws, YouTube users had been posting Viacom property, including clips from "South Park" and "The Colbert Report."

According to the Wall Street Journal, Google stated that before the end of 2006, it would introduce a new technology to recognize and filter licensed content from YouTube. However, that deadline passed without any action being taken. Viacom sued Google for $1 billion in March 2007 for "profiting from the criminal conduct of others" and willful copyright infringement.

Insiders in the media sector saw the case as a threat to force Google to reach a settlement. In an apparent gesture of goodwill, Google unveiled its eagerly anticipated content-filtering software in October 2007, indicating that it saw the Viacom litigation as a serious threat.

One last note: Our advice is based on the supposition that the threat maker is an understanding, frustrated individual who wants to work with you. Investigate your options for dealing with a negotiator carefully if threats appear to be one of her go-to strategies.

HOW TO WIN BUSINESS NEGOTIATIONS

When getting ready to bargain, don't forget to consider the corporate negotiating process. According to studies, when negotiators feel the process was fair, they are more pleased with the final result. Don't leave the course of business negotiation to chance if you want to maximize satisfaction and develop a solid working connection. You'd be prudent to think about the seven questions listed below as you engage in business negotiations with your opponent, given the significance of negotiation in business communication:

- Who is going to negotiate?

Should anybody else, such as assistants, attorneys, or other professionals, be present at your discussions in addition to you and the other party? Who will be present on each side of any team negotiations, and what position will each person hold at the table? You avoid unpleasant shocks when you jointly decide who will attend your first official meeting.

- Where will you negotiate?

Don't assume that the other side will come to you or that the other way around will happen; your opponent may have a completely different perspective on where to start negotiations than you do. You may take charge of the situation and feel comfortable when you negotiate in the workplace. However, going to the territory of the other party might show that you are serious about striking a deal and also provides you the chance to watch your rivals in their environment. Additionally, you have the option of holding your negotiations over the phone or via email at a neutral location (like a conference room at a hotel).

- What issues will you cover?

Even while you may be extremely clear about what you want to talk to your rival about, he/she might have something entirely different in mind. Spend some time making a list of all the topics you could cover as a result. Talk about how you'll handle opportunities or snags that come up during the business negotiating process, such as changes in the economy.

- What strategy will you employ?

Professionals who are attempting to negotiate commercial contracts can arrive at the table using completely different negotiating strategies. Most experts advise negotiators to approach conversations with the double objectives of producing value for all parties and asserting value for themselves in order to obtain successful business negotiation solutions. However, you might find that the opposing party had in mind a quite different strategy for the negotiation process, such as the presentation of in-depth drafts, an exchange of best-and-final offers, or a hard-bargaining contest of wills. Choose a negotiation approach that is agreeable to both parties by working together.

- What Moral Principles Will Direct You?

The majority of participants in negotiations aim to be reasonable and fair. However, depending on their viewpoint, individuals frequently have varying criteria of fairness in a corporate discussion. Additionally, we may transgress our own moral code unknowingly, such as when we excuse unethical behavior or behave badly in imitation of others. Ethical issues will appear if you make it clear that you intend to conduct yourself properly and honestly during the course of the business transaction. This might encourage everyone concerned to exercise caution while making decisions.

- How Are We Going to Seal the Deal?

It can be a good idea to talk about how you will close your final deal in advance for legal reasons. Will a verbal agreement suffice, or do need parties formally enter into a contract to demonstrate their commitment? It normally makes sense for formal negotiations to develop and finalize a written contract after a deal is reached. You should also talk about the level of authority that each of you will have during the commercial negotiating process. Will one or both parties have to make a pitch at work? If the response is affirmative, you are aware that you need to budget more time for this approval procedure. By bringing up this matter, parties can be motivated to ask their superiors for more power to make decisions with consequences.

- What Is the Schedule?

Once negotiations are formally underway, stress and confusion can be reduced by making it clear how much time each party has to come to an agreement. Knowing why someone is rushing through a business discussion may either help you to be more understanding of the need for speed or it will help you to choose a partner who has more time to spare. You might think about imposing a deadline if neither party has one in mind to ensure that the conversation doesn't go on forever. Additionally, think about making a schedule with objectives for each stage of the negotiation.

Getting right down to business, here are the top suggestions that will enable you to clinch your next big transaction, whether you're arguing for a raise or trying to negotiate a $1 million real estate deal.

> 1. First, establish a personal connection.

I cannot overemphasize how important personal connection is in negotiations. Your mood and energy will set the tone and influence the result. In other words, if you enter expecting a conflict, you will indeed experience a war. On the other hand, you're much more likely to succeed if you approach the negotiation with the expectation that you'll strike an agreement that meets the needs of both sides. It begins with a state of mind. You must let go of the notion that a negotiation is a struggle between two rivals and instead acknowledge that you are collaborating with the other party to the discussion in order to arrive at a win-win solution. You must establish a personal connection with the other party in order to get there.

Remember that it's difficult to have a genuine connection with someone via the phone, Skype, or even email. Meetings in person are always preferable.

Last but not least, remember that language—verbal and nonverbal—matters. Put a sense of shared interest and long-lasting value through by using terms like "long-term" and "common-ground." You should always be comfortable and avoid using hostile words or body language.

> 2. Be aware of who you're dealing with.

According to my observations, most transactions fail because one party lacked sufficient information about the other. You need to understand what the other side wants in order to negotiate a deal. You must actually get to know the other party's background, needs, and motives in order to understand this. What drives them? What motivates them to get out of bed each morning? Why do they stay up at night?

How do you get there, then? There is no quick fix. You need to do your homework and start by asking lots of questions. People's propensity to believe that the other party is precisely like us, that their internal logic is the same as ours, and that they have the same needs, concerns, and motivations as we do, is a prevalent error that I constantly see preventing progress. Understanding their perspective will enable you to speak to them in terms that have meaning for them and will better equip you to adjust to the conversation when terms shift.

> 3. Include more issues to discuss during negotiations, not fewer.

Not asking for more than the bare minimum is another error I observe people making. The main motivation behind this is fear; the concern that if you ask for too much, the other side may become offended and the agreement may fall through before it really has a chance. However, this concern is typically exaggerated, and if you don't bring your deal breakers to the table, one or more of them will be put on the cutting room floor.

Here is one instance. Ask for numerous additional, acceptable improvements when you are negotiating with your landlord to have your apartment painted, such as new landscaping, a new dishwasher, or new kitchen flooring. Asking for more provides you with tradable goods and wiggle room until you reach the decisive factors. You'll have a greater chance of obtaining your goals.

However, there is always the chance that you will be granted your requests.

4. Give as much information away as you can.

Having knowledge fosters trust. People grow suspicious when you play your cards too close to your chest. To convey the whole range of your thinking, be as forthcoming and open with individuals as you can. This will only make the outcome you want seem less strange.

Details support believability as well. They show that you've done your research, considered your options, and are approaching negotiating from a considered, logical standpoint.

If you're negotiating a commercial real estate project along the ocean, be prepared for inquiries and incorporate thorough details on the development's environmental impact. Make sure the disclosures, of course, align with your objectives, but don't be hesitant to lean toward openness.

5. Incorporate as many intangibles as you can

All of the legal and financial elements of a deal are sandwiched between intangibles. Why do I use the term "intangibles"? These are the items that are important to the other side and that you can give with ease; they have almost no drawbacks for you but a lot of benefits for the other party. Offer to manage social media campaigns for the opposing party if your brand, for instance, has a sizable social media following. This won't cost you much, but it will appeal to a spouse who doesn't have a lot of social connections.

In another instance, if you're an employer negotiating a pay, think about including flexible scheduling, remote days, and other intangibles. These are very beneficial to the employee, yet at little to no expense to the employer.

6. Keep in mind that life is not all about making money.

All of us would benefit from keeping in mind that money is just a form of exchange, a simple stand-in for basic necessities. Don't assume that for everyone, money is the be-all and end-all, it isn't. This is particularly evident in the millennial age, the majority of whom place a higher value on their time, experiences, and general quality of life than they do on money. If you find yourself in a bind, consider your priorities and see if they don't include money. Is there anything else except money that the other party values? Focus on anything that would be simple to concede.

7. Take small steps.

Many individuals find it difficult to cope with the hurt of initial rejection. They enter with the expectation that they must immediately hit a home run and close the deal in one day. They give up after the first rejection.

Progress is frequently modest, and the agreement may take six weeks or even six months to complete. Don't immediately try to hit the fence. Accept gradual improvement and continue moving the conversation along.

8. Use deadlines cautiously

Most people believe that deadlines aid in difficult talks, but this is not always the case. Instead, they sometimes increase irrationality and impatience and are more likely to ruin the agreement before it even starts. Deadlines might make things appear more scarce but not always. Sometimes, they frequently have the exact opposite result, making the side trying to impose the deadline appear hopeless. Depending on the rapport already built during a business negotiation, deadlines might make the communication transactional, and mere transactions are the opposite of what good deals are about in certain kinds of business.

9. Don't be afraid to think big!

Lastly, ask yourself if your thinking is expansive enough. Sometimes closing a contract isn't enough. What else was there to be done? Could there have been a connection to the back end? Once more, the confidence that comes from having a solid understanding of the other party is what matters.

Ask with confidence for what you believe your concept or product is worth if you know it will benefit their business. Never expect to receive anything you don't ask for. Go for the bakery instead of just the cake!

Putting everything into action:

These are suggestions that will enable you to negotiate effectively. It's frequently just as crucial to keep in mind what to avoid doing. Be sure to stay away from these typical mistakes:

- Don't assume that other people think the same way you do.
- Determine the other party's motivations by showing genuine empathy.
- Don't take the phrase "it's simply business" at face value.
- The expression "all business is personal" is frequently used as justification for treating people unfairly.
- Avoid overusing leverage and power. This reduces the negotiation to a simply transactional one, which is typically detrimental to both sides.

Below is an example of a business negotiation where the seller having experienced disappointments from buyers buying on credit, decides to make a better bargain to suit her interest, and avoid the disappointment that comes with sales on credit while retaining her customers:

Jane was aglow with hopes and excitement, she's about to make her first sale for the day. As soon as they tossed bargains back and forth till they met somewhere in the middle, she breathed out and said to Estelle, her customer and a familiar face who lives the next street off from hers. Their relationship had gone from strangers exchanging pleasantries whenever Estelle made past Jane's jewelry shop, to a customer relationship.

"Since we've reached an agreement of $600 dollars for the jewelry set, I would like to package it right away for you Estelle." Jane said eagerly to her.

"Yes, but there's just one issue my friend," Estelle said a little warily.

"What could that be?" Jane asked, her heart rising, she suspected a dreadful request was about to ensue.

"I do not have the money right away. However, I would pay you as soon as I can. You can have my phone number and contact address so as to assure you I'm within reach."

"I'm sorry Estelle, but giving out my goods on credit simply means that I'm giving out both my profit and capital, I cannot afford to risk it at the moment, a few of my customers are yet to clear their debts." Jane said quite frankly.

"Don't you trust me?"

"Of course I do, do YOU trust me?"

"Why not?"

"Then perhaps I should keep your item while you make installment payments for it. You can redeem your item once payment is fully made." Jane suggested prudently. Estelle paused for a moment, rubbing her chin in thought "That's fine by me," she finally agreed "at least it doesn't take a big toll on my income since I have to settle in bits."

"Absolutely!"

"Can I pay $60 per week for ten weeks?"

"I intend to have the sale of this item sealed in no more than a month which means you are to pay $150 per week." Jane said plainly.

"I'm afraid that would take a toll on my income." Estelle complained.

"Six weeks is the best I can extend to, so I'm afraid I would only accept a minimum of $100 weekly with an initial payment now."

"That sound like a deal." Estelle said contentedly and pulled out a $100 note from her bag to make her first payment.

Takeaway lessons:

- Learn to politely say no to transactions or requests from friends and family that are detrimental to your business during the negotiation phaand se, make them see reasons why it will affect your business growth.
- To combat credit defaulters, introduce installment payments on your own terms, of which item would be released after payment is fully made.

Better still here's another way to negotiate for maximized profit when a customer requests for purchase on credit:

Jane watched as Estelle caressed the jewelry piece with her slender fingers admiringly. "How much will you be willing to sell this piece?" Estelle asked.

"$800 by any means of payment asides from cash down."

"What does that mean?"

"Are you paying cash right now for it?"

"No, I intend to purchase it on credit."

"It'll cost $900 and we can negotiate the weekly installment payment. However, you can pay $600 for it, if you're paying cash now."

Estelle raked through her hair with her fingers in thoughts. *If I can save $200 from this transaction, I would be more than happy.* She thought. "I'll pay $600 cash then."

"Deal."

Takeaway lessons:

- Increasing the prices of the item to be purchased on credit will discourage customers from buying on credit.
- Lastly, avoid over familiarity in business, and set your boundaries with family and friends because most times, it is not strangers who buy on credit, it is family and friends.

REAL ESTATE NEGOTIATION

Real estate negotiating takes a lot of practice, yet certain properties don't actually require it: When you submit an offer with earnest money, it is either accepted or rejected. However, many are negotiable, making the ability crucial. Even in a seller's market, a buyer's agent will need to assist their clients in finding a property at a price they can afford. To increase the buying price over the list price, a seller's representative will need to bargain with potential purchasers. Intense negotiations will be encountered even by individuals whose main interests are in commercial real estate and real estate investing You must be able to negotiate well if you want to represent upscale properties, venture into commercial real estate, or advance your career in any other way.

Whether you're attempting to buy an investment property or sell a luxury residence, let's look at some of the most efficient real estate negotiating methods that have benefited me in my career and will undoubtedly help you, as well.

1. Be knowledgeable

You need to be completely informed on the property and the surrounding area before you even start negotiating. The comparables for this house are all substantially greater, the agent claims. Ist das so? You wouldn't know unless you looked up the facts yourself. The more information you have on your side going into a negotiation, the better equipped you'll be, and the simpler it will be for you to determine whether you're receiving a decent bargain. Keep in mind that discussions for real estate often move extremely swiftly. Never let yourself get unprepared for a scenario.

2. Allow them to initiate discussion.

The most typical negotiation strategy is not to be the first to list a number in many sectors. You don't really have that luxury in real estate, though. You require a listing price if you are assisting with a sale. When assisting a buyer, you must make an offer price recommendation. But during the bargaining process, you ought to give them the floor. You can see from their words how committed they are to the current arrangement and how easily they might be persuaded to change their minds.

3. Always have a contingency plan

A real estate transaction is really a hostage negotiation if you don't have a contingency. It's important to have a plan B. If you're representing a seller, you should have other offers down the pipe. If you're representing a buyer, you should have other houses they're interested in. It's hard as an agent; you're not representing your own interests. You're representing someone else's. You have a fiduciary duty, so that means you can't negotiate against your client, even if your client could be better served elsewhere. So, your negotiation skills begin outside of the negotiation process by giving your seller or buyer more options. If your seller or buyer feels backed up against the wall, then you may not have been doing enough to represent them.

4. Be Willing to Leave

Being ready to walk away during a real estate deal is one of the most crucial pieces of advice. However, as was already noted, the most important thing is to make sure that your buyer or seller is prepared to back out because, unless you're buying or selling for yourself, they are ultimately in charge. Spend some time conversing with your client. Real estate agents must inform their clients on the options available and what they should or shouldn't do as part of being skilled advocates. In a market when there are no buyers at all, prospective buyers must be practical. If your clients could wait until the following year, you wouldn't want them to be robbed since while it could put money in your pocket now, it will later harm your reputation.

5. Recognize the strings you can pull.

Does the purchaser worry about closing costs? Is the seller concerned that they will have to undertake improvements or repairs? During the course of real estate negotiations, speak with the opposing agent to ascertain what is and is not significant to them. It's possible for a listing agent to state up front that the seller will cover closing fees. In contrast, a buyer might need to be more precise; perhaps they are worried about closing costs due to the high price of the home, but what they truly need is any kind of concession. Knowing more gives you more negotiation power. You'll eventually get a sense for individuals and what matters most to them.

6. Pay attention to the feelings involved

Emotion and money play equal roles in the sale of a home. Never lose sight of this whether bargaining with a buyer or a seller. If you're a selling agent, be aware that if it's their "dream home," a potential buyer might be more willing to spend extra. If you represent a buyer, be aware that a seller can be persuaded to sell if the buyer matches their preferred criteria, such as a young family. Financial exchanges alone do not constitute a negotiation. There is no set cost for the asking price. Always talk to everyone involved and concentrate on what matters most, which is if all sides are at ease with the transaction. Many transactions have been influenced by a handwritten note rather than monetary compensation.

7. Display decency and respect.

Real estate is not the place for shady deals, but there are other places. You'll interact with other agents in your region on several occasions. You want to get along well with them and avoid developing a negative reputation. Even though you must be a tough negotiator, you must still have good manners. As well as letting them tell you what they need, let them know what you need from the deal. Learning how to politely reject an offer is a necessary component of improving your negotiating skills.

8. Always do in-person negotiations.

A text-based negotiation cannot be successful. Real estate negotiations should ideally take place in person, if not then over the phone. Simply said, most negotiation techniques don't translate well into text. Even if the agreement is a good one, it's far too simple for the other party to second-guess themselves. When you bargain face-to-face, you can infer more from the other person's demeanor and movements. Confidence and body language will help you become a better negotiator.

9. Avoid bargaining against yourself.

Starting a negotiation with yourself can easily happen. Why does that matter? You put up a purchasing proposal, but you see that the other side isn't responding. As a result, you return to your client and inform them that you don't believe they have accepted it. We must ascend further. However, you haven't yet received a "no." Acting uninterested while one is actually interested, is a typical real estate negotiation strategy you should familiarize yourself with.

Similar to this, a customer can try to persuade you to reduce your real estate commission by demonstrating disinterest and patiently waiting for your response. Never try to get a better bargain for yourself or your client by negotiating against yourself.

10. Make an effort to find common ground.

In all likelihood, you and the other party are interested in the same outcome: the contract closing. This is something that you should use in your negotiation technique. Establish common ground. Both of you want the house sold. Both you and the other agent are curious about your commission percentage. Similarly, even though you might want them to accept your opening offer, you are aware that they desire a counteroffer. However, you are also aware that everyone at the negotiating table needs to be pragmatic. Either it's worth that much or it's not.

The most successful negotiators are actually problem solvers who understand that both house buyers and sellers ultimately want the deal to close – with the fewest number of issues as possible.

RELATIONSHIP NEGOTIATIONS

Whether you are trying to negotiate your way into a person's life as a close partner or you are in the brink of getting started with a relationship or caught in the middle of its ups and downs and you need to negotiate your way around getting what you want from it, these negotiation tips for relationships will help you get things fixed up.

1. Before entering a situation, anticipate what you want from it.

Choose your top objective for what you most want to happen in a situation, whether you have seconds or days to do it. You now have context. If not, you risk projecting your own worries onto the other person. You are then less able to be totally present, to listen, and to be flexible and open. When this happens, people often react instead of making a decision on how to behave. Additionally, you are able to realize that you wish to shift your primary aim more quickly. When we are speaking with someone we have already interacted with frequently, like a spouse or coworker, this strategy is very helpful. It enables us to stop repeating negative language patterns from the past and other habits.

2. Recognize that, often, less is more

Keep your movements and voice slower and lower, listen more, and say less, especially at first. The likelihood that people will feel more secure and comfortable around you is increased by these behaviors.

3. Slow Down To Speed Up

When you initially meet someone and when you see them again, move and speak more slowly and indirectly. Allow them to feel heard and to "own their area." Later, you can move more swiftly and directly.

4. Behave as though everything will go well for you.

You are more likely to finally bring out their more positive side if you focus on their positive intent, even when they initially seem to have none.

5. Take a step back to consider how another person would perceive the situation. In various circumstances, particularly hostile ones, we frequently:

- Pay attention to the positive aspects of our behavior and the negative aspects of theirs.

- Assume that they are acting as they would if we were acting similarly when they do something.

These automatic reactions may lead to miscommunication and an intensification of the dispute.

6. Consider the interests of the other person first

Use the Triangle Talk method of speaking to connect, which emphasizes mutuality-boosting mindsets: first, discuss their interests (theirs), next how the topic links to a sweet spot of shared interests (ours), and finally, discuss your interests (me). The likelihood that the other person will listen to you for a longer period of time and feel as though you are considering their requirements while making your proposal is higher.

7. Take action to allow the other person to save face and make amends

You have a better chance of keeping the relationship intact if you do this. Instead of accusing someone of misrepresentation if you believe they are lying, keep probing them with questions (until you lose control or run out of creative ideas). By asking inquiries, you can potentially save face by having time to determine whether you were mistaken. If your suspicions turn out to be true, by politely enquiring rather than criticizing them, you are giving them the opportunity to admit a mistake or misunderstanding and preserve their face. They are then more inclined to make the necessary adjustments. In case they refuse to accept their mistake, you also give yourself room to escalate later.

8. Focus on shared experiences rather than highlighting differences.

The focal point of your relationship will be whatever you discuss the most regularly and passionately. Refer to the parts of them and their arguments that you can agree with and want to develop more.

9. Don't rely on their being able to see the image you are presenting.

Don't assume the other person will see all the advantages of what you are suggesting. Spend some time vividly describing the advantages to them in their own words.

10. Never offer anything you can't accept.

Make an offer you can live with even if the other person

accepts it rather than playing a bluff. Don't, for instance, include anything in an offer that you anticipate the other party will find unsuitable and reject. It's possible that you misread the scenario or the person, and you discover that they do accept your offer.

11. Essentially make the same offer, but in a different way

Never rule out the prospect of rearrangement of an offer's same components to arrive at a more agreeable compromise. For instance, when it comes to money, take various payment schedules into account.

12. Remain mindful

"You have to be present to win," as is the rule for many competitions. Keep your feet on the ground and focused on the now, only looking back and forward for context and balance.

13. Take into account how you'll be expressing yourself.

For instance, a priest once requested his supervisor whether he might smoke during prayer, but the request was denied. However, he may have obtained a favorable response if he had asked if he might pray while smoking.

14. Make and Uphold Agreements

The more you take the initiative to help bring about a win-win agreement, the more likely it is that you will increase their trust and encourage them to behave similarly in the future.

NEGOTIATIONS IN MARITAL DISCORD

Negotiation can be used to settle a lot of marital disputes. We're talking about leveraging the same types of quid pro quo deals that happen whenever two parties, no matter where they are, are at war with one another. Although it may seem strange to discuss negotiation in the context of a close relationship, it works pretty effectively. In actuality, happily married couples negotiate a lot with one another. A husband might exchange sexual favors for household chores, or both partners might decide to alternate doing what they both prefer. Negotiating well enables for both parties' needs to be met, which is what makes it so beneficial for solving marital issues. Here are things to bear in mind while negotiating during marital discords:

- Negotiation is not compromise, to be clear.

    In a negotiation, each party receives something in return for providing an item that their partner wants. Neither party genuinely gets what they desire when a compromise is reached. They frequently choose a middle ground between two extremes of a problem, leaving neither party happy with the resolution. Imagine a situation where two people were going out to dinner and one preferred Middle Eastern food while the other preferred seafood. They eventually come to an agreement to have pizza delivered. In other words, neither party received what they desired but neither was made to do something they didn't want to, thus they can't be entirely happy with the outcome. One spouse would choose the restaurant this time, and the other the next, in a negotiated solution.

In many ways, negotiated agreements are superior to compromises. In exchange for giving something their other really wants, each partner receives what they really want. Each individual can feel that they are being treated fairly and equally in the connection. Additionally, they have the chance to feel as though they are contributing to the relationship, which increases their sense of commitment to their spouse. Additionally, they tend to treat one another better and feel better about their relationship because each partner also feels better about the other. Both parties need to be aware of their agendas for a negotiation to be successful. You must be aware of what you are bargaining for and avoid getting distracted by unrelated matters. We all have a list of requirements and desires for a partner and a relationship. This list is known as our agenda. We are merely acting in our own best interests when we negotiate by being aware of our agenda and using that as a framework. We cannot properly negotiate until we are fully in touch with our own needs and aspirations.

- We must also make every effort to clearly and concisely communicate our position in order to engage in effective negotiation.

It's ideal to phrase issues in terms of what our spouse does (behavior), rather than who they are, if there is something we'd like them to change (personality). As an illustration, you can agree to disagree on how money is spent, but you cannot agree to disagree on your partner's lack of financial responsibility, just as you cannot agree on their height or age. Furthermore, describing a problem in terms of personality can be interpreted as an attack on our partner's character, which may prompt them to do the same to us in return.

- When presenting a topic, keep the conversation focused on that particular problem.

Sometimes, couples will use a single argument as an outlet to vent their unhappiness and dissatisfaction with their relationship as a whole. It appears as though there is a large sack carrying all the unresolved problems. The entire contents of the bag are thrown onto the ground and upon one another when a problem arises. Consider a scenario where a couple receives two invites to supper on a Saturday night. The argument heats up as they try to determine which one to accept, and one of them says to the other, "You always insist on having things your way. You have the same stubborn nature as your mother.

To this charge, there is no suitable retort. If you're stubborn, there's not much you can do to change that right now and whether or not you got this trait from your mother is irrelevant; comments of that nature just serve to inflame rage. It's important to note that because you are no longer discussing the initial issue, negotiation is impossible because the conversation has veered off course.

- Barter agreements make for the most fruitful negotiations.

There is a significant possibility that your partner wants something from you if you want something from them. If you list a few items you'd want to get and a few things you're ready to give in exchange, it will be simpler to find a solution. Remember that the fundamental tenet of a negotiated settlement is that we receive something that satisfies our wants while also providing for the requirements of our partner.

The answer must also be acceptable to both partners and must have been reached after careful consideration of each other's ideas, views, feelings, and values. Each partner must feel that their choice was their own and not imposed on them. The issue cannot be resolved by pressuring a partner into consent or giving in before feeling genuinely comfortable. The truth is that a genuine compromise will end a problem. Sometimes we may believe we have struck a compromise only to discover that the same problem reappears later. That typically indicates that one or both partners did not fully agree with the final choice. You can stop running into the same issues once you and your partner are happy with the solution.

- You must maintain an open mind during the negotiation process and be prepared to hear what your spouse has to say.

If you want to develop the relationship in the correct way, you must understand that they may have valid reasons for what they are doing or saying that you find undesirable. Each partner has a distinct and valid view on the matter, and this should be respected by all parties. Without respect, you cannot engage in equal-footing communication or truly consider your partner's viewpoint. Additionally, avoid trying to negotiate when you are angry (e.g. anxious, angry, etc.). It is better to wait until everyone has calmed down before you start the process because while our emotions are high, we tend to think less clearly than we should and we tend to be more reactive.

HOW TO WIN PUBLIC AUCTIONS

An auction is when many parties want the same thing, and they are set against one another. As they are all brought together, they bear in mind that only one, who bids the best price, will get what they want. This can be used to encourage competition between buyers and sellers.

In a typical auction, bidders present increasing prices until no one else does. In a Dutch auction, a price that started off high was reduced until the first bid, which sealed the transaction.

People will want something more when they are aware that they could miss out on it. We are inherently competitive creatures, and when faced with rivals who desire the same thing, the focus can shift from acquiring the object to simply dominating the rivalry. This is what happens at auctions when two bidders begin competing and bid well above the item's actual value.

It might be challenging to resist the allure of outbidding the opposition during intimidating auctions. But if you have a solid auction plan in place, you'll be in a strong position to win your dream house when the hammer falls—without paying too much. Even if buying a house at an auction might not be your first option, there are several advantages for you as the buyer.

For a bidder ready to pay market value, auctions can be effective since the item is certain and yours when the hammer drops. Private sales always carry the possibility that the seller will decide otherwise or accept another offer before you have a chance to haggle. You can observe your rivals and understand your position in an auction.

Winner's curse

The winning bid in an auction has a tendency to be higher than the item's inherent value or genuine worth, which is known as the "winner's curse." Incomplete information, strong feelings, or a number of other subjective elements that may affect bidders are commonly to blame for the difference between the intrinsic value and the value realized at auction. As a result, the winner will either be "cursed" in one of two ways: either the winning bid will be higher than the asset's value, making the winner worse off overall; or the asset's value will be lower than the bidder anticipated, leaving the bidder with a potential net gain but a worse situation than they had anticipated.

The important thing to remember is that winning the auction means negative news for the winner about the item's worth. It indicates that the bidder was overconfident and that too much was paid if, on average, the bidders' estimates were accurate. Therefore, knowledgeable bidders lower their ex-ante estimations to account for this effect. With more bidders, the winner's curse becomes more severe. This is due to the likelihood that some bidders will have underestimated the worth of the object being auctioned as the number of bidders increases. Oil firms may estimate an oil field's value to be anywhere from $5 million and $20 million if, for instance, it has an inherent value of $10 million.

The corporation that miscalculated its value at $20 million and bid at that level would win the auction only to discover that it was actually worth less. This is why auction negotiations are unique and require tactics pertinent to them.

Despite the fact that each auction is unique, there are several tips you can use to start strong and hopefully win:

1. Delay posting your first bid

Often, it is best to wait until the bidding has begun and then place a strong bid. This gives you the opportunity to assess the competition, and determine when the property will go on the market (once the reserve price has been met), and it also helps to weed out bidders who are merely looking for a deal.

2. Set a strong first bid that reflects the market values

There's little use in starting off too low in today's transparent world when property valuations and estimates can be accessed on bank applications and the like.

Everyone present at the auction will know exactly how much the asset is worth and will have arrived at the event prepared to pay that amount, just like you. It's best to start close to where you want to finish so you can quickly eliminate many of the low bidders. Make your opening offer count.

3. Offer including rounded figures

It's better to steer clear of placing bids with odd figures, like $649,500, as someone will inevitably pay an extra $500.

Go in with an even number rather than a negative one, and if your rival tries to slow down the bidding with minor increments, go in above them with that extra $500 or so to put yourself back in the lead right away.

4. Enter with a counter bid that is confident and quick.

After another bid is received, placing your own immediately shows that you are serious about the situation and will also enable you to see who your rivals are.

5. Contact the agents

Although it may be alluring to blend in and remain invisible, it's crucial that the real agent and auctioneer notice you and recognize you as a serious bidder.

You can always rely on agents to help you navigate the process, so it's important to keep them informed without divulging too much. Many times, disgruntled buyers blamed the agency and said things like, "I would have paid more if I had known it was going to sell for that much," yet they were evasive when the agent asked for information.

6. Decide on a budget and hold to it

One of the major mistakes purchasers make at an auction is failing to establish and adhere to a maximum price they can pay.

In the end, regardless of how much you may fall in love with a house or how close you may feel to winning, you should never go over your budget.

TACTICAL SALARY NEGOTIATIONS WITH EMPLOYERS

The truth is that learning tactical payment negotiation methods and avoiding the landmines of salary negotiation are essential to getting the job offer you want and deserve, regardless of your experience level with job-hunting or your love or loathing of the art.

Salary negotiating is no longer only a savvy job search tactic as the discussion over pay fairness continues to gather steam. In fact, it is increasingly becoming a sign of empowerment and self-advocacy. However, if we're being completely honest, pay negotiations aren't always the empowering discussions we'd like them to be. They can also be extremely nerve-wracking. However, knowing how to request the pay you deserve can increase the likelihood that you'll really get it.

Salary negotiations can be uncomfortable, just like any crucial conversation. The majority of people's unease stems from dread. You may be worried about the following if you are going to discuss your salary:

- Being unsure about how to begin a discussion
- Picking the incorrect moment to negotiate
- Choosing the salary to request

Being calm and confident is the first step in the most fruitful pay talks, but getting there can be challenging. Remember that many businesses will be willing to pay you a wage that is roughly 20% more than that of your current company (as long as you bring the proper talents to the table, of course!), which should bolster your confidence. To advocate for yourself and earn the pay you deserve, start with the following advice:

1. Understand the purpose behind your request.

Be sure to do your study on the going market rate whether you are negotiating the wage for a new position or revising the salary for your current one. In addition to geographic area, candidate experience level, industry, and other considerations, companies also use market rate, or the average wage that other employers pay employees in positions that are comparable to theirs, to determine compensation.

When deciding on your wage request and your justifications, keep these variables in mind. One obvious reason to negotiate your wage is that you desire more money, but you should also think about other, more focused factors, like:

• Paying for higher personal expenses

• Increasing your ability to earn money

• Outlining your contributions to the workplace.

• Matching your salary to your increased level of experience, education, or training

• Matching your salary to a change in your job responsibilities (e.g., additional workload)

Knowing what motivates you to have this conversation will help you remain composed and confident; even if you choose not to share your motivations with your employer (which you are not required to).

2. Don't reject yourself.

You know that inner voice that discourages you from negotiating your pay? Please disregard that. Even while it may seem safer to talk yourself out of negotiating, doing so is almost as bad as having your boss reject your request for the compensation you deserve. Give yourself a chance to express your desires. If you never inquire, the response will always be "no," as the saying goes.

3. Don't pardon yourself.

It may seem like asking for a favor when you request the wage you want, but it's not! As an employee, you have the right to request the pay you deserve. Saying "sorry" during a negotiation or other attempt at self-pardoning is equivalent to denying that you truly believe you deserve the compensation you are seeking. Other expressions to steer clear of that could convey the same impression are:

- "I realize I don't have a lot of experience, but..."
- "Maybe now isn't the ideal time to inquire..."
- "Despite the fact that I don't have everything you need"

Although you should negotiate with clarity, professionalism, and knowledge, you do not have to modify your request to be more agreeable to your employer. Don't feel guilty about asking for the pay you want.

4. Give it some time.

Have you ever been so anxious or doubtful of yourself that you spoke without pausing to catch your breath? This happens frequently, especially when you just want to finish the task at hand. Nevertheless, it's crucial to take your time when settling on a pay. Explicitly state what you require. Whenever necessary, take a break.

If you normally speak quickly, work on slowing down by

refraining from filler words and phrases like "I mean," "like," "essentially," and "you know," concentrating on one topic at a time, and pausing for a breath before you speak.

5. Embrace the silence.

The moment after you've asked for extra money, there may never be a quiet as loud as that one.

Your boss might be debating whether to accept your offer, pondering a strategy to buy some time until they're prepared to respond, or, if they're disoriented, they might be considering something completely unrelated.

In any case, you should fight the impulse to talk throughout every pause. Even though silence can be uncomfortable, you are not required to speak. Instead, accept the stillness as a necessary step in the process. After you've presented your case, give your boss or supervisor some time, even if it's just a few seconds, to answer. A level of confidence that employers frequently find appealing can also be communicated by demonstrating that you are at ease in quiet.

6. Get some practice in with it!

There may be room for some practicing because you won't become perfect and prepared overnight. Practice your speech while allowing your thoughts and ideas to flow naturally. Just in time for the conversation with your supervisor, practicing can help you develop your skill.

You can practice in front of the mirror or record yourself on your phone to see how you present. Just as crucial as rehearsing your words is improving your body language, facial gestures, and posture.

Do your third practice session with a friend if at all possible. Have a friend play the role of your employer as you practice the negotiation with them. Request some questions from your friend or accept a challenge to get through an unusual circumstance. For instance, if you find it difficult to communicate with someone who are obviously distracted, ask your companion to pretend disinterested while you are negotiating. This will enable you to devise a strategy for getting around it while conveying your point.

Practice as much as you need to in order to become more composed, assured, and at ease when making your request.

10 sample conversation dialogues for salary negotiations in every situation

You still need to come up with some strategies for being more composed and self-assured before you can negotiate your pay. To assist you in navigating the dialogue, review these scripts. Each can be easily changed to suit your particular circumstances, and you can even combine them if necessary.

The majority of these scripts are written as though you will be speaking to your manager since in an ideal world, you will be able to negotiate your wage face-to-face. If you intend to email your request to your employer, you can modify these scripts to a written form —this is likely to be particularly typical for prospective employees who have been mostly communicating with the possible company via email while negotiating a new employment offer.

1. You're haggling about a new wage.

"Good day, Jermaine. Once again, I appreciate you extending the Developer I position. I'm overjoyed with the prospect of working for XYZ Company. But before I accept your offer, I'd want to ask for a wage in the region of $80,000 to $85,000 since it corresponds to my training, experience, and education as well as the going rate for this job."

2. You're revising your present wage.

"Again, I appreciate you coming to see me today. I've worked with the company for three years, as I indicated in my email, and over that time I've taken on more duties as we've lost several team members. Recently, in addition to my responsibilities as a purchasing assistant, I was asked to take on the position of purchasing manager. Before I agree to that, I want to evaluate my present pay and come to a figure that is commensurate with the new responsibilities I've been requested to take on. This position had a salary range of "$106,000 to $110,000" earlier this year. The amount of money I think makes the most sense for me is $108,000."

3. Initially, you agreed to the offer, but you later changed your mind.

It's crucial to remember that sometimes trying to renegotiate a salary you've already agreed to can work against you and the company might even withdraw the job offer entirely. But if you change your mind about the pay you initially agreed to and want to bargain, this script can enable you to do so without jeopardizing your job offer.

"I have had some time to further examine the position since initially accepting the job offer that came with a salary of $50,000, and some fresh information has emerged regarding what is necessary for the work. I'm still interested in the job and am prepared to start when we originally agreed, but I'd like to renegotiate the pay for a range of $55,000 to $60,000. Do you think this would be a good range to settle on today?"

Give yourself the best chance of success by implementing the following supplementary advice:

• Don't make any other changes. The start date and job title you agreed to are still valid.

• Reiterate your enthusiasm for the position and the

organization. Inform them that you intend to stay for a while and that you just want to make sure you're happy before accepting the position.

• Have a plan for everything. Your company may agree to the extra pay you want, reject it, or offer it to you at the expense of another benefit (e.g., taking away your hybrid work schedule in exchange for the increased salary). Be prepared to properly answer by attempting to foresee their various responses.

• Don't procrastinate. Most businesses move swiftly to complete the hiring process once you accept an offer so you can begin working. Don't wait to renegotiate for more than 24 hours.

4. The "Gratitude Sandwich" is being used.

What is the best aspect of a sandwich? In the same manner, it begins and finishes. This script is built on the premise that every sentence should begin and end with "thank you."

"I appreciate you considering me for a position on your team. Even though I was already a great fan of the DEF Company brand, going through this process has given me even more insight into your staff and heightened my enthusiasm for working for your company. Although the offer for this position is smaller than I had anticipated, I would gladly accept a salary of $95,000."

5. You've received a lowball.

"Thank you for delivering the Senior Business Analyst position offer. Starting with cleaning up your current business requirements to produce improved efficiency, I'm convinced that I may be a valuable addition to your team.

I want to look through the suggested salary before I accept your offer. I mentioned in my interview that I have thirteen years of experience in the fintech industry, five of which were spent working for a huge company that functions quite similarly to this one. I have managed a high-performing team for the last eight years that has routinely exceeded their goals by 10%, which will be very helpful to you given the individual in this job would be in charge of two sizable teams. I'm looking for a salary of between $160,000 and $170,000 considering my background. What options do you have in this price range?"

6. The offer is inside your salary range's lower end.

If you don't intend to accept the lower end of the range, you might be wondering why you should provide a salary range rather than a single number. Giving a pay range gives you and the employer flexibility to negotiate a salary that works for both of you. However, here's a little-known fact: Nobody actually wants to be at the low end of their range.

It shows good trust on the side of the employer to meet you halfway by at least offering the middle of your range. If they only make an offer at the lower end of your price range, they may just be doing it to entice you to accept the position. Go for it if you think you'll be content with that sum in the long term. However, if you choose to reject the offer, here's how to do it:

"I genuinely value your adaptability. I would like to get as close to the top of my wage range as possible based on the value I would be delivering to your company and the MBA I recently got, which exceeds your educational criteria for this position. I would feel most at ease receiving $90,000. What would be required to raise the offer to more closely match that wage?"

7. You lack all of the prerequisites.

If you have three of the five mentioned criteria for the position, are you still eligible to negotiate your pay? Yes, in a resounding way! In all honesty, there are no perfect applicants, and even necessary qualifications aren't always necessary. So you should still bargain even if you don't have all the necessary qualifications. After all, the company has already demonstrated that they genuinely desire you for the position by making you a job offer while being aware of your qualifications. As you bargain, keep this in mind, but don't focus on what you don't have. Instead, concentrate on your strengths, particularly if the company has highlighted them in the job description.

"Thank you for giving me the chance to interview with you. I appreciate the offer. I've previously worked for a health and wellness firm, as you said in our interview, so I am familiar with the demands of a startup and totally committed to helping you with your rapidly shifting business needs. In light of this, I'd want to counter your $35,000 offer with $45,000. At that salary, would you be able to accommodate me?

8. Your written offer is less favorable than the one made orally.

Imagine this: You've already had the verbal offer for the fantastic job you were hoping for, and now you've finally gotten the paper offer—but the pay is less than they promised. Verify whether there was a mistake on their behalf as soon as possible. If it is, fixing it should be straightforward. But if it's not, you might have to bargain. Employers may occasionally modify their offer after reviewing your wage history; in these situations, a prospective employer will use your present income to estimate what your new salary should be. Here is how to respond if the company has dropped the offer due to the compensation review (or for another reason):

"I can see why you revised the promised wage in light of fresh information. My requirements, however, have not altered, and I continue to possess the knowledge, expertise, and training required to succeed in my position. In order to reach the first wage offer of $55,000, I would like to negotiate the salary."

Wait for the written offer before discussing your wage as many firms make verbal employment offers before presenting written offers."

9. You prematurely stated the intended salary.

Early in the hiring process, an employer may ask you what pay or range you're seeking. The employer might hold you to it by supplying that precise number toward the conclusion of the procedure once you've given it to them. There is nothing else you need to do if you decide to stick with it than accept the offer for your new employment! If, however, throughout the interview process you learned new details about the position, you might wish to revise it. Even if the requirement for frequent travel wasn't disclosed in the job offering and you discovered it afterwards, you are still completely within your rights to negotiate. Here's an illustration:

Since you provided the sum I first suggested, I can see you've been paying careful attention throughout this process, and I appreciate that. I've discovered certain extra needs that weren't mentioned in the job description during this process, such the need for travel. My ideal compensation for the position has changed as a result. Given this new information, I would feel most comfortable accepting a salary in the range of $55,000 and $60,000.

10. You detest bargaining.

Since it's easier said than done, many women continue to shun compensation negotiations completely. In fact, 57 percent of women who responded to a Randstad survey claimed they had never bargained with a boss, and 60 percent indicated they would quit their positions to earn a higher wage somewhere else. Even so, haggling over your pay can help you get the money you want and establish an important precedent for asking for what you want, even if it means having a difficult or uncomfortable conversation. It's usually a good idea to advocate for yourself in the job, and that includes negotiating your compensation.

Address the issue at hand to reduce any tension. This is how:

"I understand that bargaining can occasionally be uncomfortable for both parties, but I do want to emphasize that standing up for my rights improves my performance at work and on the team. When I have everything I need to succeed at work, including remuneration that is fair and commensurate with my expertise, I am better able to contribute significantly not only to my team but also to the business as a whole. According to my study, a compensation range between $79,000 and $85,000 is more appropriate for my job and for this stage of my career. How can we collaborate to accomplish this?

Although you can modify these pay negotiation scripts for various scenarios, you'll note that they always end with a "thank you" for the offer. This is due to the fact that showing gratitude is a crucial component of any negotiation and can aid in developing a rapport with your rival. Each script also specifies a specified pay or salary range, as you'll see. This is one of the most crucial aspects of the negotiation, along with showing thanks. Never request a "better wage" and then demand the employer define what that means. At every turn, be precise and explicit.

DEALING WITH COUNTER REACTIONS DURING SALARY NEGOTIATION

However, it would not be a walk in the park if you worked for someone like my previous boss or a harsh human resource manager. You should be ready for his counterarguments intended to discourage you from negotiating your wage. Before you approach the negotiating table, analyze his thoughts and respond to his statements. Here are some of the elements of a difficult employer's conversation you might anticipate and how you should react to it.

#1 Dialogue

"Do you honestly believe that your performance deserves such a wage increase?" the HR Manager asks.

What tactic does the HR manager have when they say that?

• To make you feel uneasy

Candidate would probably respond by saying:

"Yes, the amount of work I do for this organization has increased over the years, but my pay has never been raised, and by having me put in more hours, you were able to avoid hiring a new employee."

What should the candidates' approach be?

• To persuade the HR Manager of your qualifications and name example

What an applicant SHOULD respond?

"I am absolutely certain. I successfully completed one of our most crucial projects last month (example of your impact). I firmly believe that I merit a pay raise because of this.

HR Manager says in Dialogue Number 2:

"I'm sorry, but the business's financial situation at the moment does not really permit that."

What tactic does the HR manager have when they say that?

• To demoralize you

Candidate would probably respond by saying:

"I completely agree, yet in my previous company, by implementing software X, I was able to raise client satisfaction by 3% and observe increased productivity. Through the business, 10% of the annual budget might be saved."

What should the candidates' approach be?

• To demonstrate sympathy and provide a concrete example

What an applicant SHOULD respond?

"I am aware of that. I'm open to discussing new services in lieu of raising my pay. Coupons for food, a business vehicle, a gym membership, etc."

The third dialogue's HR Manager says:

"If I pay you more, then your coworkers will all request compensation increases as well."

What tactic does the HR manager have when they say that?

• To turn you away

Candidate would probably respond by saying:

"I am able to talk for myself alone and like to do so. I firmly believe that a pay raise is something I have earned, especially in light of my expertise and recent accomplishment, which helped me land the future project as well."

What should the candidates' approach be?

• To concentrate on your accomplishments and examples of successful projects

What an applicant SHOULD respond?

"I promise not to discuss our arrangement with any of my coworkers. It is none of my business what you talk about with my coworkers because we all have separate responsibilities. I'm here to discuss how I performed (Give an example)."

Fourth dialogue

HR Manager declares

"I'm stuck on my salary pay decision. If it were up to me, I would offer you a pay raise, but our CEO is in charge of that. And they will undoubtedly choose not to."

What tactic does the HR manager have when they say that?

• To build pressure

Candidate would probably respond by saying:

"I recognize that. I've told you about my experience and value-added. If you told our CEO about that and advocated for me to get my pay raise, that would make me pleased."

What should the candidates' approach be?

• To find allies

What an applicant SHOULD respond?

"You are the one who knows my qualifications and the value I provide to the organization the best because you are my direct manager. Which pay raise do you believe is appropriate?"

Utilizing these examples will aid you while negotiating salaries; rehearsing them beforehand will improve your wage negotiation abilities.

SALARY NEGOTIATION MISTAKES YOU SHOULD AVOID

While there is a lot said on salary negotiating strategies, I would like to turn my focus on negotiation tactics you want to avoid, specifically salary negotiation blunders that could lead to a significantly lesser job offer or, worse yet, the loss of the job offer you worked so hard to secure. By heeding the suggestions below, it will be simple to avoid these 9 blunders.

1. Not negotiating/Settling:

The biggest error you can make is to just accept the first deal you are given and settle. According to research, female and younger job seekers frequently make this error due to either a lack of understanding of the negotiation process or a dislike or discomfort with the idea of negotiating. You'll earn less, receive smaller increases (since most raises are calculated as a percentage of your income), and have a lesser pension if you settle for a lower pay than you are worth (since pension contributions are usually a percentage of your salary). But accepting a job offer that, in your heart of hearts, is too low will not only cost you money, but will also gnaw away at you until you finally start to truly resent your employer and/or job. Of course, it goes without saying that you should haggle over your pay in some occupations (like sales).

2. Concentrating on want or greed instead of value.

Focusing on what you believe you need or deserve during pay negotiations instead of your value and the value you provide to the potential employer is a very typical mistake. Employers don't care if your wage won't be enough to pay your rent, mortgage, school loans, or even living expenses. If you intend to haggle over a job offer, do it on the basis of thorough research (see following mistake) and a convincing case for why you are valuable to the company. Never mention to the employer that you require a specific pay.

3. Poor preparation for negotiations or research.

There is no justification for you as the job seeker to be unaware of your market value given the abundance and range of wage information available online, including professional associations and websites like http://salary.com and www.salaryexpert.com. Of course, you should also make an effort to examine the historical wage levels, negotiating procedures, and performance evaluations of your potential company. You will have a greater understanding of the market for your services and your value in that market, even if you opt against negotiating salary.

4. Making an early salary proposal.

The more authority you have, the longer you wait. However, a lot of job applicants approach the hiring process too early and inquire about pay and benefits. When you are the last applicant remaining and have received the job offer, then is the optimum time to discuss wages. At that time, you can enquire further about the salary, incentives, commissions, health insurance benefits, and other perks. Asking earlier in the process may be seen as being overly preoccupied with money; it may also force you to disclose what you are willing to accept.

5. Quickly accepting a job offer.

These days, finding a job takes forever, so when you do receive an offer after weeks (and in some circumstances, months), it's not uncommon to want to accept it immediately. Even the best offers should be considered when you are calm and unburdened by the gaze of your potential employer or HR director. The majority of firms are ready to allow you a few days to a week to think over the job offer. Because the employer has chosen you, you have the most power when you receive a job offer. Make the most of this authority to ensure that the position and job offer are right for you, and think about negotiating for a higher offer if you believe it should be available. Just keep in mind that you have that amount of time—or whatever it is—to make your choice.

6. Rejecting a Job Offer Too Soon.

When an employer offers a salary that is far lower than anticipated, many job searchers reject job offers quite fast. While in many circumstances you would be justified in doing so, it is still preferable to give the offer some thought before declining it outright. You might be forced to decline the offer if the compensation is simply much below average. Consider the advantages more carefully if the pay is adequate but just not as adequate as you would want. Rejecting a job offer too fast without considering the total remuneration package is a big mistake. For instance, some businesses with lower salary give higher incentives, stock options, or health insurance at no additional cost. Additionally, keep in mind that you ought to be able to negotiate one or two aspects of the offer to strengthen it even further.

7. Requesting excessive changes in the counteroffer

If the offer is not what you anticipated but you have a strong interest in the position and the company is a good fit, you may want to consider making a counteroffer proposal. It's critical to keep in mind that you can only discuss one or two of the offer's most crucial components if you decide to submit a counterproposal. If the pay is too low, emphasize it in your counteroffer. If you know the employer won't address the compensation, concentrate on modifying a couple of the other terms of the offer, such as more vacation time, earlier performance reviews, a signing bonus, and relocation costs. Just keep in mind that you cannot try to negotiate the entire offer; instead, you must pick your battles wisely, do your homework, and craft a brief counterproposal.

8. Personalizing Salary Negotiations

Always conduct yourself professionally when conducting the negotiations during this procedure. You are the finalist for the job if the employer has given you an offer, so even if discussions fail or worse, remember that you did receive an offer, even if it was not what you wanted or deserved. You should never burn any bridges, so if discussions with the employer end in a deadlock, do so gently and extend your gratitude for the opportunity once again.

9. Not requesting a written final offer.

When all is said and done, and you have accepted a job offer, the last thing you should do is request a written copy of the final offer. If your employer refuses to put the offer in writing, accuses you of lacking trust, or otherwise tries to pressure you into accepting the verbal agreement, take this as a big red flag that something is terribly wrong.

Extra tips for salary negotiations:

1. Consider Perks and Benefits. These may all be paid for with a low wage, and they include better insurance plans, flexible

days off, personal development budgets, the option to work from home, and better retirement savings plans.

2. Support your argument. Your abilities, experiences, and skills should support your counterproposal.

3. Leverage Your Situation, third. You can use your unemployment as a negotiating chip if the position you're applying for will pay you less than its rival or your existing company.

4. Recognize when to stop or leave. Don't press the issue if your employer is obviously uninterested. If the job offer makes sense, accept it, otherwise politely decline it.

5. Pick a Range (And Pick the Higher Number): If you heed the advice of the day and include a wage range, the hiring manager will almost always offer you a salary that falls at the lower end of the range. Set the terms by choosing the larger number as the starting point for the negotiation.

6. Act graciously and likeably; avoid appearing combative and uncooperative during talks. Keep emotions out of the argument and base it on facts.

7. Make it evident that you want the job by emphasizing your enthusiasm for both the organization and the role. Indicate that, despite having employment offers from other companies (with higher compensation), you still prefer this one in order to prove you aren't just in it for the money.

NEGOTIATION SKILLS FOR CAREER WOMEN

The documented experiences of women in the labor market in the past, shows that even the most skilled and well-prepared negotiator might have her plans derailed by unforeseen events and invisible hurdles. Women frequently struggle during compensation negotiations because of this. When women self-advocate for salary increases at work, they frequently find themselves in the unpleasant position of having to "juggle while they are on a tight rope."

Gender discrimination is frequently implicit rather than apparent in the United States. The fact that it still exists in the workplace, however, poses a personal negotiation issue for women, forcing them to balance their requirements with the way they communicate those needs to their counterparts. For this work, a more "measured approach" is necessary.

Although pay negotiating abilities can be used in a variety of situations, the majority of negotiation literature and study focuses on women in compensation negotiations, neglecting the impact of negotiations on their career path and lifetime earnings.

Several suggestions for women on how to negotiate pay:

1. Planning

-Keep track of your contributions to the company and your supervisor's feedback.

-Find mentors and sponsors to assist you in advocating for your professional goals.

2. Investigation

According to research on negotiations, women do better at the negotiating table when they have access to objective information before a pay-raise negotiation, such as salaries of peers and colleagues in the same industry.

-Investigate salaries that are comparable in your industry and among your peer network.

-Connect with both male and female coworkers inside and outside of your company to assist you build your arguments for a raise with factual evidence.

3. Purposes

According to female salary negotiation study, women need to justify their demands during a negotiation more frequently than men do.

-Consider the situation from the standpoint of your employer.

-When requesting a compensation increase from your counterpart, say "we" instead of "I."

4. Style of Negotiation

You must be able to read your counterpart's emotions in order to predict their next move during complex negotiations. The likelihood that the female negotiator's intentions and words will be misunderstood will be reduced if she refrains from using email and other electronic communication methods.

5. Watch Out for Outside Offers

According to research on negotiations, aggressive tactics used by female negotiators frequently fail. While negotiation specialists might typically encourage a negotiator to leverage outside offers to sway the outcome of discussions at the bargaining table, this strategy may harm a woman's chances of negotiating her compensation. If you plan to bring up a third party offer during your pay negotiation, be careful how you word it to avoid your counterpart taking it as a threat.

6. Advantages of Negotiation Simulation Role Playing

With the help of negotiation role-play simulations and practice sessions with a neutral adversary, strong pay negotiation abilities can be strengthened. This can assist negotiators of both sexes in honing their message and how they convey their case. You will be better able to foresee and resolve any challenges that may occur during the actual salary negotiation by strengthening your case for your pay increase and taking advantage of the chance to see the various problems from your counterpart's viewpoint.

CRISIS NEGOTIATION SKILLS

(Business Crisis, Robbery, Hostage, Violence)

Extensive business crisis management plans are frequently created by organizations. Whether the crisis entails a building evacuation, a drop in the company's stock price, or a product recall, an organization can promptly and effectively transition from day-to-day operations into crisis-management mode through a quick, centralized response.

What is crisis management in negotiations, why is it necessary, and how can your business navigate a crisis successfully? Professional hostage negotiators have offered solutions that can assist individuals handling a business negotiating crisis and we found that these curated list of steps also works during any nature of crisis which includes violence, robbery, hostage etc. we therefore have gone ahead to identify the characteristics present in most crisis negotiation.

Crisis-related negotiation traits

What does negotiation crisis management entail? Similar to a hostage negotiation, a commercial crisis negotiation typically consists of the following characteristics:

* High stakes, requiring communication to diffuse a difficult situation.

- Business negotiators might not know how a problem will develop, much as hostage negotiators don't know what a hostage taker will do next.

- Intensified feelings. Negative emotions frequently peak in tight circumstances.

- Multiple parties and teams; People frequently lash out and aggravate the situation. Complex crisis talks frequently include the involvement of numerous teams and entities.

Seven steps to crisis negotiation success

Business negotiators handling crises should find the following five tested hostage crisis negotiation strategies helpful. Some of the tips are police negotiation techniques collected from the NYPD Crisis Negotiations Team.

1. Get ready for a crisis.

The use of crisis management plans benefits organizations. Discuss the potential for a dispute to arise during the term of your contract with a potential new business partner, as well as how you might resolve it. You may, for instance, include a provision stipulating that you meet frequently to go over any issues that have arisen and how to resolve them. You might also insert clauses in the contract requiring mediation between the parties before filing a lawsuit as a means of resolving disputes.

2. Ascertaining the source of the occurrence (s)

An occurrence that precipitates a crisis is the final straw or the catalyst. As was previously stated, the precipitating event frequently entails a large loss or reversal (e.g., spouse, job, money). Because it identifies the dispute that has to be resolved during the negotiation process, determining the precipitating event is essential in setting the foundation for problem solving.

The person in crisis is frequently perplexed by the effects of the precipitating incident because of the initial high levels of emotion. But in order to successfully negotiate a solution to the problem, these are the hooks that the parties will utilize.

A scenario that law enforcement might run into, for instance, involves a dejected subject whose ex-wife has notified him that she plans to take full custody of their children and deny him visitation. In response, the subject locks himself and the kids inside his house and won't let them out or come out. The projected loss (of the children) is the obvious bait in this situation, and the negotiator needs to identify and focus on it. Then, the subject's activities are positively reframed by offering explanation (and minimizing hostile purpose) for this behavior (e.g., You aren't doing this to damage your children in any way; You're doing this out of your love and care for them; You're trying to protect them). This reduces internal conflict, diffuses negative feelings, and prepares the environment for future issue solving and crisis management.

2. Establishing a dialogue and building rapport

In the end, those who can express their feelings in precise terms are better able to find solutions to their issues. Thus, it is crucial to carefully listen to the person in crisis during crisis intervention. A listener (negotiator) is seen as understanding when they are able to represent the subject's feelings (see Active Listening Skills below). This is the foundation of a partnership where the party in crisis is willing to take the negotiator's advice and do so, ending the crisis.

3. collecting intelligence

This has to do with the continuous evaluation of the crisis situation to:

(a) Determine the lethality or possible harm to the individual in crisis (and others),

(b) Identify precipitating events,

(c) Create suggested action plans and post-crisis solutions (such as counseling, medical follow-up, and imprisonment). Using communication, intelligence collection is performed. While the individual is in distress and by conducting interviews to learn more about their history (friends, coworkers, relatives) and record checks (criminal, civil, medical, psychological).

3. Lay down the ground rules.

If you do find yourself in the middle of a crisis negotiation, such as a disagreement over a delivery delay, give yourself some time to set the ground rules before you start having real discussions. You might advise, for instance, that you make a formal commitment to being truthful and to keeping your word. FBI crisis mediators assert that being truthful will help hostage negotiators win the trust of hostage takers. Trust can be built on the basis of ground rules, and they also provide you the freedom to refuse unreasonable requests. When they feel they are being treated ethically, hostage takers are more inclined to accept a denial of their demands, according to hostage negotiators.

4. Face your feelings head-on. Since the majority of hostage situations are fueled by intense emotions, hostage negotiators have created successful techniques for controlling such emotions. Officers of the hostage negotiation squad for the New York Police Department, emphasize the significance of paying close attention to a hostage taker's demands in order to determine his major underlying issue or purpose. Typical hostage-taking tactics involve calming the hostage-fears taker's by using active-listening strategies including self-disclosure, paraphrasing, and encouraging comments. Similar to this, business negotiators handling a crisis need to keep in mind that it is never a waste of time to probe the motivations behind a counterpart's stated stance.

4. Buying time

The greatest ally of the crisis negotiator is time. The passage of time alone typically lowers stress and emotional levels, and hostage-takers' strong emotions have a tendency to de-escalate with time, which creates the conditions for fulfilling the objectives of crisis intervention. In the world of law enforcement, buying time is referred to as verbal containment or the method of keeping the distressed individual occupied by having ongoing conversations with the negotiator. Don't hasten the procedure. Business negotiators frequently believe that a negotiation in a crisis situation ought to be completed as soon as feasible. You might presume that you need to strike a solution quickly if someone is threatening to go to the press if you can't come to an arrangement, for instance. Surprisingly, hostage negotiators suggest that we proceed slowly with our talks. The greatest strategy in a heated scenario is typically to go methodically.

5. Calming intense emotions

Two levels of communication are present. The first level concerns the story's or content's underlying facts as told by the speaker. The second level of interaction focuses on the emotive response to the story is known as emotion, which is how the reader feels about the story or (as she just stated). The emotional response and subsequent behavior are what lead to crisis as opposed to the real occurrence. A communication level assessment is carried out by considering the content and feelings associated with utterances, one may communicate the same information but adding distinct emotional undertones. I HATE YOU!, on the other hand, might convey rage while I HATE YOU! might convey contempt. Since a person's feelings about a situation will greatly influence their conduct during crisis, it is important to detect and deal with any negative feelings.

6. Make the connection stronger.

According to veteran NYPD police commander Robert J. Louden, when a police negotiator tells a hostage taker, "We're in this together," he is not just saying it for show. Instead, the negotiator is attempting to forge the kind of connection that will enable the parties to work together to find a solution to the situation. Similar to this, in the business world, their problem is also your problem; therefore concentrate on working together to come to a solution that works for both of you.

One of the most difficult scenarios you will come into as a negotiator is a crisis negotiation. All negotiators can benefit from adopting the mantra of the NYPD negotiating team: "Talk to me" during these difficult times.

7. Problem solving

The subject is more likely to be open to problem solutions once emotions are properly managed, communication has been established, and the triggering event has been identified and discussed. In a multistep behavioral process known as problem resolution, the negotiator aids the individual in crisis in exploring options and practical solutions. Crisis negotiation problem resolution is an adaption of the following procedures outlined by behavioral experts over the past few years:

- identifying the issue

- generating ideas for potential remedies

- removing inappropriate remedies

- selecting a course of action that the negotiator and the individual in need deem acceptable.

- organizing the execution

- executing the plan

Listening for skewed cognitions from the individual experiencing the crisis is a necessary component of effective issue solving. The way a person thinks affects how they perceive themselves and their environment.

The world is viewed through the lens of cognitions. Additionally, they affect an individual's response to events, wherein flawed, dysfunctional, or irrational thinking may lead to emotional crisis or distress. Sometimes these misconceptions interfere with the ability to solve problems, thus the negotiator must address them.

Example of crisis negotiation:

Illustrative is the case of a drug addict who attempts to steal a prescription medication from a drugstore but is caught. Before he can flee, the police are called and surround the building.

His eyes darted all around the store as he heard the loud blaring of sirens and the lights from the police vehicles flashed colours of death into his eyes which were the only thing seen beneath his mask, he was suffocating in panic, the mask was suddenly too tight, too hot – he was a masked criminal in a drug store who's about being busted. "Darn my addiction!" He cursed. "What?" the frightened lady beside him thought he had spoken to her, her fingers trembling. "Never mind." the drug store staff were assuming their position despite he had them froze with the pointing of his gun, now they were summoning their courage; the police was here after all. He grabs a kid and points his gun at the side of his head, the boy winces in fright as the cold metal touches his skin and he begins to cry "Mummy...mummy"

The police break in.

"Drop the gun now!"

His eyes darts around, they were trooping in from different direction. "Shit", he muttered. The boy's mother sobbed aloud.

"Please let him go"

The criminal wouldn't listen. He eyed the police men and weighed his options.

"Set me free now, or I will kill the boy."

"You will go to jail, you are not yet a murderer, your jail term wouldn't be a life sentence yet, you only stole, now don't make things worse, set the boy free."

On hearing that, he thought of the possibility that they wouldn't want to back down, knowing he wouldn't pull the trigger either and put himself in a life sentence mess – an added penalty to his crime; it all made sense to behave rationally. He released the boy who quickly ran to his mother.

His fears still overwhelmed him – he was certainly going to jail, not a life sentence but he was going to spend years in the box and that was his biggest dread; incarceration. He pointed the tip of the gun to the side of his head.

"I don't want to go to jail. If you don't set me free I'll kill myself at the spot." His voice was shaky.

The chief negotiator among the police had his gun pulled out as well like the others but he had to water down the tension and help eliminate impulsive moves "You don't have to die, you have an option. You're going to be sent off to a drug rehabilitation rather than prison. Put the gun down now."

Here, the negotiator breaks, the erroneous assumption is that there are only two options: being set free or going to jail and responds by presenting another option: the potential for being sent to drug rehabilitation instead of prison (which may or may not be a reality). The individual eventually gives up without additional incident. The subject's perspective has changed as a result of the negotiator's suggestion, and a better course of action is now apparent.

The above methods can be used in terrorist and organized criminal negotiation as well; however, there are more things to keep in mind. First is to understand the nature of terrorism and organized criminals and the reasons for negotiating with them at all. Note their motivation and goals along with the expected outcome of such negotiations, also note the format such negotiations should ideally take.

NEGOTIATING WITH TERRORIST ORGANIZATIONS AND ORGANIZED CRIME

Politicians in the US and the UK have been saying "we do not negotiate with terrorists" on a regular basis for decades, claiming that doing so is both ethically wrong and unworkable because it would likely inspire more terrorism and legitimate its goals. There is a moral case against governments bargaining with terrorists. For instance, paying ransoms aids terrorist organizations in keeping control of a region, pays its members, and encourages more terrorism and hostage-taking.

Some contend that the millions of euros spent by France, Germany, and Spain for the release of their citizens have greatly strengthened Al-Qaeda in the Islamic Maghreb, which is accountable for a number of kidnappings in Algeria.

'Negotiating with terrorists promotes further acts of terrorism'

The idea that the best approach to discourage terrorists from taking hostages is to remove the motivation is the foundation of the "do not engage with terrorists" position.

According to this notion, terrorists will stop considering hostage-taking as a feasible method of raising money or gaining concessions if nations unite around the idea of never paying ransoms.

However, some seasoned negotiators hold that governments must engage in negotiations with terrorists; that by doing otherwise, governments are merely rehashing outdated ideas; and that as a result, lives are sacrificed needlessly.

It cannot be demonstrated that refusing to negotiate with terrorists deterred or prevented the kidnapping of US and UK people or made it easier for them to be released. Even though it is morally dubious, paying a ransom does frequently succeed in returning people home safely.

Negotiating with dangerous criminal organizations is a real possibility. Governments, the police, community leaders, religious leaders, and criminal organizations all engage in it. Even some of the negotiations have legitimate aims or ambitions. However, the majority of the efforts remain undiscovered, either because they were carried out in secret, out in the open, or both.

It is significant to highlight that the term "terrorist" in this context does not always have a clear definition. Although several Mexican drug cartels clearly terrify local communities, the FBI has, for example, permitted private corporations to negotiate the release of hostages abducted by these cartels because they are not considered terrorist organizations.

We will look at how to deal with two different types of unconventional armed actors: 1) "violent extremist" groups like jihadists, and 2) "violent crime" organizations like mafias, gang networks, pirates, and drug cartels.

The motivations and expectations behind why governments or other actors negotiate:

- A feeling of moral or religious obligation

- Concern about members of criminal organizations

- Compassion for the impacted community

- Temporary cease-fire and cessation of hostilities

- Disarming and demobilizing

- Collaboration between law enforcement

- Eliminating the group's covert nature

- Restoring public services and utilities

- Exposing secret cemeteries

- The eradication of certain crimes like forced recruitment and extortion.

One of two strategies typically prevails when government or state entities are formally involved in conversations with criminals: direct but secret talks or dependence on one or more reliable third parties.

Negotiations with criminal organizations may fail, result in unfavorable outcomes after implementation, or create moral hazards along the road, but this does not mean that they should be disregarded as a strategy for reducing crime and violence from the start. The continuation of worn-out, ineffective law enforcement strategies that fail to stop violence, condemn communities to systems of criminal violence and governance, and fail to adapt creatively to changing conditions can result in issues that are equal to or worse. Negotiation can be a powerful technique for minimizing the violence associated with criminal organizations if it is effectively planned and executed.

14 Examples from real-world situations of the most varied and fruitful series of discussions with criminal organizations:

1. Bangladesh - Pirates of the Sundarbans: In 2016, a local journalist oversaw a mediating process in the Sundarbans in response to community demands for a decrease in pirate violence and harassment. The journalist had to travel back and forth between meetings with the heads of the pirate group and the Bangladeshi government. Through him, the government made judicial and financial inducements available to the pirates in exchange for their surrender of their weapons and cessation of their violent and illegal actions. Following the negotiations, a number of pirate gangs disbanded and openly turned in their firearms, which reduced crime, abduction, and piracy while also improving the living circumstances of the surrounding villages. However, the government has only partially fulfilled with its obligations, and legal action is still being taken against the pirates. Other organizations carried on with their operations and violent behavior.

2. Belize - Multi-Gang Truce: At the beginning of September 2011, after several days of discussions, a truce was agreed between government representatives and thirteen gangs in Belize City. The gang members were given social and financial incentives, including job prospects, in exchange for agreeing to stop the violence. Short-term violence decreased significantly as a result of the agreement, but after a few months, public outcry increased, donor support dwindled, and government funding for the pact ran out.

3. Brazil – Gang Violence in Prisons: Gangs in Brazil have long organized violence from within jails and prisons. Several have grown into significant global drug trafficking operations. The state and gang

leaders engaged in negotiations after numerous bloody jail riots in the states of Paraná and Amazonas in 2014 and 2017, respectively. Prison conditions improved, and there was a temporary decrease in violence.

4. Colombia – Pablo Escobar and the 'Extraditables': During the years 1990–1991, Colombia negotiated more forgiving conditions with Pablo Escobar, the head of the world's cocaine trade, and other criminals. The government consented to amend the laws to prevent the extradition of traffickers to the United States and permit Escobar to serve his term in a jail he could remodel in order to lessen the harsh and crippling violence that he and his colleagues, Extraditables caused. It requested that he stop his violent campaign against the government in return. The pact was able to endure even the scandal of Escobar's escape from his specially designed prison because to the prevalent sense of desperation toward the Extraditables across the political spectrum.

5. Colombia – Gulf Clan Negotiations: Colombia engaged in negotiations with the Gulf Clan, a drug trafficking organization made up of former paramilitaries and guerrillas, also known as Los Urabeos, in 2017–2018. A justice agreement was the proceedings' main goal. Acting from a position of relative institutional strength, the government rejected the suspension of extradition the cartel requested, but participated in protracted discussions regarding a variety of other potential legal leniency options. The contentious procedure sparked a lot of criticism and strong spoilers, and it failed to produce a deal.

6. Denmark – Motorcycle Gang Truce: A journalist asked a defense lawyer to mediate a peace between

two motorcycle gangs, the Hells Angels and the Bandidos, after an unprecedented surge of inter-gang violence between 1994 and 1997 resulted in the deaths of twelve gang members and more than 70 injuries. Authorities in Denmark accepted the mediation, which was seen as a crucial step in putting an end to the "Nordic Motorcycle Gang War." On national television, the truce's establishment of peaceful dispute resolution procedures was announced. Following implementation, gang attacks were permanently stopped.

7. Ecuador – Gang Legalisation: Two levels of negotiations were involved in this case: local and national. The first occurred in Guayaquil in 2006 when the local police helped to arrange a peace agreement with the Latin Kings and the etas to lessen the level of violence. After a short while, the national government started a discussion process that, as part of a greater shift in policing and public safety, culminated in the legalization of both organizations as youth cultural associations after two years.

8. El Salvador - Mara Truce: In 2012, the government secretly arranged a ceasefire between violent Maras (gangs) in exchange for a reduction in their criminal activity. Iron-fisted law enforcement was largely seen as having failed, and gang confederation was blamed for the majority of fatalities in the nation. In the end, the government agreed to better jail conditions, gang member transfers, socioeconomic packages for their rehabilitation into society and for community improvement. However, some of the terms of the agreement were not met by the parties, and when the agreement was made public, there was a tremendous political backlash. As a result, killings fell by 52% in a

year. This resulted in a breakdown in execution and a rise in violence, among other things.

9. Honduras - Mara Truce: In May 2013, the Mara Salvatrucha (MS-13) and Barrio 18 gangs publicly declared a truce in exchange for a future negotiated path of reintegration into society, with early support from the government. However, the government changed its mind about its alternatives after homicide rates rose right after the declaration, and the talks broke down.

10. Haiti – Bargaining with Gangs: From 2000 through 2010, two NGOs engaged in repeated negotiations with criminal groups. One only sought entry to gang-controlled areas so that they could safely deliver aid and medical attention. It concentrated on establishing its own credibility among the local populace and threatened to cut off services if assaulted. The conversations were successful, which had the side effect of lowering local violence. The second NGO attempted to negotiate a purposeful reduction in violence using material incentives, but was unable to produce long-term behavioral change after the material incentives were removed.

11. Italy - Trattativa Stato-Mafia: As part of a bigger plan to battle mafia organizations, the state implemented legal changes in the late 1980s that affected how mafia members were prosecuted and treated in prison. As a result, 338 of the 475 alleged Cosa Nostra members who testified in a "maxi" trial were found guilty. As a result of the mafia's retaliation against members of the government and civic society, an unprecedented wave of terror was unleashed. Members of the Special Operative Forces

of the Carabinieri (i.e., the national gendarmerie) allegedly engaged in negotiations with the Cosa Nostra leadership in an effort to lessen the current wave of violence. When the government condemned this, judges put some of the key negotiators to prison and labeled their actions as criminal corruption many years later.

12. Jamaica – August Town Truce: In 2008, after a 24-day negotiating process mediated by the Peace Management Initiative (PMI), a national non-profit organization advocating non-violent dispute settlement, the leaders of six separate gangs in Kingston's August Town neighborhood signed a truce. Law enforcement personnel at the local and national levels were aware of the negotiations and openly backed the final agreement. Despite occasional inter-gang disputes, the cease-fire persisted for three years before it was broken and the bloodshed started up again.

13. Spain - Gang Legalization: In 2003, the Barcelona city government hired academics to do a gang analysis as a result of the growing territorial conflict between the Latin Kings and the Etas. Their investigation showed that rather than organized crime organizations involved in serious illegal activity and severe violence, the gangs were primarily made up of immigrant youngsters with a strong sense of cultural identification. The academics were then given permission by the Catalan government to begin a transformative negotiation process, which resulted in the gangs' official legal recognition as cultural groups. Both are currently legally recognized organizations, enabling their members to benefit from educational and

socioeconomic opportunities and prevent tense encounters with law enforcement.

14. Timor-Leste - Martial Arts Groups: In the decades after Indonesia's occupation of East Timor in the 1970s, several regional martial arts organizations imitated the organizational forms of violent gangs and grew more and more involved in illicit activities. A peace building program to lessen violence by such groups was started in September 2006 by the local organization Yayasan Hak, the international NGOs Concern and Oxfam, and the regional NGO Action Asia. Members of the martial arts clubs participated in a one-year peace-building course as part of the effort, which was led by Action Asia and the partner organizations. A peace agreement was reached between the two main groups, officially putting an end to their prolonged conflict. Although tensions between them remained high and fights occasionally took place, this helped to lessen the bloodshed.

The motivations and expectations behind criminal Groups' negotiations:

- Legalization, like in the case of Maras in El Salvador;

- Safe passage for group members or members of the community they control through hostile territory (example: discussions in Pakistan's Lyari Town);

- A brief halt to hostilities (like the gang truce in Jamaica);

- Employment or an apprenticeship (such as bargaining in Belize);

- Legal leniency (ex., discussions between the Urabeos and the

Colombian government);

- The right to form groups (such as Pandillas in Spain);

- Better public services for marginalized populations (for instance, in Brazil, talks with gangs);

- Recognition of culture and identity (example: martial arts gangs in Timor-Leste);

- An end to humiliating arrest methods (such as those used by Norwegian motorcycle gangs);

- Possibilities for education and training (such as the Latin Kings and the etas in Ecuador);

- The cessation of extradition (ex: Colombia's talks with the Extraditable); and

- The cessation of arrests or the weakening of organizations and regulations aimed at combating crime (e.g. the Trattativa Stato-Mafia).

In a negotiation, it is plainly essential to fully grasp the intentions and expectations of a criminal organization. However, the goals will frequently change as the discussions continue on, whether as a result of internal pressures, emerging expectations, or tactical changes.

Numerous Starting Points for Negotiations with Criminal Organizations

The state may or may not start negotiations between criminal organizations or between them and the government. But frequently, they are started by an outsider. It is remarkable how frequently, and sometimes without any engagement from the government, a single, well-intentioned third party—such as an activist, a religious figurehead, an academic group, an NGO, or even a lone police officer—provided the impetus in the cases under examination. It was a journalist with knowledge of the area who recommended the method and served as its architect and facilitator in the negotiations with the Bangladeshi pirates. Religious officials took the lead in the situations of the gangs in Guerrero state (Mexico) and the Gonzalez neighborhood in Port of Spain (Trinidad). A criminal defense attorney quickly emerged as the primary player in Denmark's mediation with motorcycle gangs, but in both cases in Haiti, NGOs initiated the conversations with local gangs. Women frequently played a hidden role in talks and had a strong influence.

Format and management of negotiations with terrorists and organized criminals

Planning can make a big difference in whether a complex negotiation is successful or unsuccessful. Process design is frequently seen as just technical and hence unimportant, yet it is necessary for a successful negotiation and the chance of a final agreement and execution. In fact, the parties should spend just as much time and attention on the planning and management of the negotiation as on the actual issues being discussed. Some of the essential elements of good design include:

- Outlining the negotiation's final goal in clear terms;

- Deciding on a concise and limited agenda as well as a set of procedures;

- Specifying the make-up of delegations as well as the venue and frequency of negotiations;

- Planning for strong technical and operational support teams and knowledgeable assistance;

- Supporting bilateral and unilateral initiatives to boost confidence;

- Defining the scope and function of any facilitators, mediators, and guarantors; and

- Establishing protocols for any public involvement or external communication, as well as internal confidentiality.

GOVERNMENT AND POLITICAL NEGOTIATION

The main alternative to using force or dishonest tactics in statecraft is diplomacy; this is how complete national power is utilized to the peaceful resolution of problems between states. It may be forceful (supported by the threat of using force or punitive measures), yet it is clearly peaceful. Its main methods are discussion and negotiation on a global scale, which are primarily carried out by authorized envoys (a term borrowed from the French envoyé, meaning "one who is sent") and other political figures. The majority of diplomacy is carried out in private, in contrast to foreign policy, which is typically announced in public. However, in modern international relations, both the fact that diplomacy is underway and its outcomes are virtually always made public.

War may break out when diplomacy fails in a heated chaotic situation, yet diplomacy is still helpful in times of conflict. It guides the transitions between protest and threat, conversation and negotiation, demand and retaliation, and conflict and peace with other governments. Coalitions that prevent or start war are formed and maintained through diplomacy. Enemies' affiliations are broken up, and potentially hostile powers' passivity is maintained. It orchestrates the end of battle and creates, bolsters, and upholds the peace that follows conflict. The long-term goal of diplomacy is to create an international system that encourages enhanced state collaboration and peaceful dispute resolution.

The main actors in diplomacy, though by no means the only ones, are diplomats. They are experts at relaying information, negotiating changes in relationships, and mediating disputes between states and peoples. Their weapons are words, backed by the authority of the nation or group they speak for. Leaders can build strategies and tactics to influence the behavior of outsiders, especially foreign governments, by understanding the attitudes and behaviors of those in other countries. The secret to a successful foreign policy is the effective employment of diplomats.

We may learn from the highs and lows of some of the most well-known public discussions, regardless of the nature of our talks (commercial, legal, regulatory, internal, etc.). Government talks about economic strategy are ongoing and extremely public because the Euro is in serious problems and economies around the world are shaky.

Example 1: The US negotiations over federal budgets, taxes and spending

The US is scheduled to implement (or expire from) a number of key tax and spending provisions in December and January, so official Washington will be wrangling ferociously at year's end. The fate of the US national economy, the US government's credit rating, and the American people's faith in their elected officials' capacity to address significant issues are all at stake, and the stakes could not be higher.

President Obama and Speaker of the House John Boehner of Congress came very close to reaching a "grand bargain" on long-term debt reduction during negotiations. It paired higher taxes on the wealthy with curbs on the expansion of entitlement programs, two issues that are important to the Democratic Party (which is anathema to the Republican party). However, the transaction collapsed at the final minute. Examining this unsuccessful negotiation's components through the lens of best negotiating techniques may offer insight into what may occur at the conclusion of this year as well as advice for our everyday bargaining.

Example 2: The Chen Guangcheng Crisis

When Chinese rebel Chen Guangcheng made a dramatic house arrest escape in the spring of 2012 to the American Embassy in Beijing on the eve of the annual negotiations between the United States and China on strategic and economic issues, the Obama administration's diplomatic skills were once again put to the test.

The Chinese government insisted that negotiations between U.S. and Chinese authorities on Chen's fate be handled in the strictest of secrecy. One of the most well-known negotiators of 2012, Secretary of State Hillary Rodham Clinton, didn't bring up Chen's fate with her Chinese counterparts until after he made up his mind to leave China for the United States, and even then, she did it subtly. According to The Times, the Chinese made the decision to allow Chen to study in New York within a short period of time.

Face is more important in Asian society than any contract, this is true while highlighting the necessity for China to keep the delicate negotiations under wraps and speak only intangibly about Chen. The discussions serve as an example of the potential benefit of in international negotiations, adapting to your counterpart's negotiating approach.

Example 3: Talks with North Korea

Beginning in 2011, the US engaged in lengthy negotiations with North Korea's unstable, covert leadership. After Kim Jong-passing, Il's the protracted negotiations picked again up under Kim Jong-new Un's administration.

The nations reached a deal on February 29, 2012, whereby North Korea agreed to halt its development of enriched uranium weapons and long-range missiles in exchange for a sizable amount of U.S. food aid. However, North Korea ruined the agreement by revealing plans to launch a satellite with a long-range missile just 17 days later. North Korea launched a rocket on April 13; the rocket detonated in midair.

Some of the most renowned negotiators in the world routinely deal with dishonest opponents, and they are aware that it might be beneficial to negotiate a "test" agreement in which you only make a few concessions. However, make sure the opposing side is aware of the repercussions of reneging. Be ready for the possible repercussions of a failed bargain, including reputational harm.

Example 4: Iran's Nuclear Option

Israeli Prime Minister Benjamin Netanyahu expressed doubt that international pressure will be effective in persuading Iran's leaders to halt the nation's nuclear program during a meeting at the White House on March 5, 2012. According to the New York Times, Netanyahu allegedly warned President Barack Obama that the West shouldn't resume talks with Iran until it committed to halt its uranium enrichment programs.

Obama, a renowned and patient negotiator, is reported to have disagreed, stating that this circumstance would end discussions before they ever began. He encouraged Netanyahu to first try diplomacy and economic sanctions before considering taking military action. Republicans, meanwhile, expressed skepticism about the prospect of successful negotiations between the United States and Iran.

Example 5: The Conflict in Syria

Another of the most well-known negotiators in the world, former U.N. secretary general Kofi Annan, announced his resignation from his position as the United Nations and Arab League's special envoy for peace to the Syrian conflict on August 2, 2012. Early in 2011, a nonviolent revolt against President Bashar Assad started, but it eventually descended into civil conflict.

The Syrian government was to withdraw its heavy weapons and troops from inhabited areas, and opposition militants were to surrender their arms, according to a deal that Annan had reached. The proposal also described a procedure for Assad's replacement as part of a political transition. Assad promised to follow the peace plan, but neither his administration nor the rebels actually took action to put it into effect.

The U.N. Security Council had unanimously endorsed Annan, but Russia and China, who held the veto, resisted taking further aggressive action that may have required a change of administration by outside forces or foreign military intervention. On this subject, Russia and China were at odds with the United States, the United Kingdom, and France.

The international dispute over the agreement's terms and its implementation may have been exacerbated by inadequate pre-negotiation with Security Council members prior to the creation of Annan's proposal. The departure of this well-known negotiator serves as a reminder of how crucial it is to obtain support from one's supporters before beginning a large negotiation or dispute-resolution effort.

Program on Negotiation chairman Robert Mnookin, a well-known negotiator in his own right, suggests carefully considering the decision of whether to negotiate, including the potential costs and benefits, as opposed to dismissing a negotiation with someone you deem to be evil, irrational, or unethical on principle. Consider elements like your interests, the interests of the other party, potential alternatives to the negotiation, the nature of a prospective bargain, potential costs, and the likelihood that you can carry out a deal.

LESSONS FROM INTERNATIONAL NEGOTIATIONS AND NOTED STRATEGIES

The following negotiating techniques, which can be used to generate agreements even between parties who are skeptical, are highlighted in the examples of international negotiations:

1. Work with reputable mediators.

Without intermediaries helping the parties think and exchange proposals, a solution would not have been achievable. It might be just as useful to use two or more mediators who stand to gain from facilitating a settlement as it is to rely only on a neutral third party.

2. Evaluate your strength.

The Ukrainian negotiators understood that Russia had a lot riding on a grain agreement. With this understanding, Ukraine realized it had the strength to advance its own interests in the negotiations.

3. Be skeptical and check.

Oversight is essential to make sure parties fulfill their duties when there is little to no trust between the parties.

The UN and Turkey must keep an eye on the parties' behavior and hold them responsible for violations if the grain agreement is to remain in effect.

4. Benefit from incremental contracts.

Russia, Ukraine, the UN, and Turkey will need to communicate often in order to carry out the agreement, which might lead to increased collaboration and diplomatic successes. Waheguru Pal Sidhu, a professor at New York University, said to the Christian Science Monitor that the verification process "may eventually lead the door to something greater."

THE PSYCHOLOGY OF MASS PROTEST AS A TOOL FOR NEGOTIATION

If you've ever found yourself in the middle of a crowd, screaming words along with the rest, such as "No justice! No peace!" and all that, you've actively participated in taking several steps further from the negotiation table. Protesters marching through the streets, blockading streets and buildings, and halting traffic are not only using the last resort tool for negotiating with society and higher authorities, they are engaged in activism and activism seeks to create unease, show opposition, and draw attention to differences when roundtable negotiations have failed or have been purposefully avoided by the higher party.

But you might ask, must it come to this? Why not alternative dispute resolution (ADR) and its calm dialogues?

Keep in mind that any ADR professional is always thinking about relative power dynamics. In discussions and negotiations, power dynamics determine which sides have the most authority and influence. In the event that a negotiation fails, parties who possess a higher relative level of power typically have more negotiating leverage, more flexibility, and better alternatives. There are a few requirements that must be satisfied before any disagreement may be settled, despite the fact that ADR tools can successfully mediate conflict amongst parties with different power dynamics. Specifically, the strength of the parties cannot be so uneven that one lacks the ability to speak up during negotiations.

Activism and protests are indications that societal concerns have developed to the point where they must be broken in order to give the cause a voice after being greeted with silence and inaction. Conflict resolution rarely begins with protests. Since demonstrations are typically the final resort, in my opinion they indicate that there are structural obstacles preventing ADR from taking place. There needs to be a fundamental understanding that all sides are deserving participants with a stake in the discussion. The parties frequently are unable or unwilling to enter into negotiations if their dignity is called into question or rejected.

Protests may not be anyone's initial negotiation option or fit into all negotiations but here are a few vital things that protests can do:

- Protests give parties, groups, and individuals whose voices have been silenced by societal restrictions the ability to negotiate. Although it is frequently said that activist movements lead to tension and conflict, I think that these issues already exist and that protests only help to bring them to light in a way that attempts to provide oppressed groups a voice, dignity, and attention.

- Protests can challenge societal imbalances that, more often than not, are related to power dynamics and have prevented effective ADR from occurring. Giving the disadvantaged group authority can result in conflicts being settled through ADR because the usually more powerful party will now have to hear what the disadvantaged group has to say.

- Protests are efficient. Through ADR community conversations can be facilitated, discussions between activist leaders and local politicians and law enforcement can be mediated, and the details of how best to stop excessive use of force by the police can be negotiated for instance. But, ADR itself cannot provide a solution to the oppression or marginalization of a population. Protests are necessary. Protests confer dignity.

"When an individual is protesting society's refusal to acknowledge his dignity as a human being, his very act of protest confers dignity on him."

-Bayard Rustin

LAW COURT NEGOTIATION

Taking legal action by going to court in order to obtain justice might be helpful, although it is not the only way to accomplish your goals. It is good to think about other ways to accomplish your goals before pursuing legal action such as through mediation and negotiation as they may be faster, less expensive, and more efficient options available to you for obtaining justice.

The term "out-of-court settlement" refers to a common alternative to going to court. In an out-of-court settlement, the opposing parties to a case (or potential litigation) reach a compromise understanding. In these agreements, the party presenting (or about to bring) the case consents to drop it, or decides not to bring it in exchange for something from the opposing side (such as payment, an apology, or a behavior change).

Alternative dispute resolution (ADR) procedures are frequently used to reach out-of-court agreements. Any way of resolving conflicts without going to court is referred to as alternative dispute resolution (ADR). ADR brings together all methods and procedures for resolving disputes that take place independently of any governing body. The most well-known ADR techniques are negotiation and mediation, but there are also arbitration, conciliation, conciliation, conciliation, and transaction. It's crucial to consider these two options both before and after filing a lawsuit.

In order to reach a settlement, disputing parties will negotiate over the issues in a case.

Key elements of negotiation in the justice system:

- There is no fixed method and it is an informal process;

- It might be spoken (in person) or written;

- It can occur between the parties directly or through their attorneys;

- It typically entails both sides making "concessions" or compromises in order to come to a mutually agreeable conclusion;

- The parties have power over how things turn out. There can be no accord without their approval;

- Talking is done in a discreet and private manner. In court, they cannot be used against you; and

- The agreement made at the conclusion of a negotiation is frequently a "contract" that is enforceable against the parties.

Mediation is a process where a neutral third person (a mediator) will help the opposing parties reach a negotiated settlement (this process can also be called conciliation). This is like a negotiation but with a third party.

Key elements of Mediation in the justice system:

- The parties choose a neutral third party to serve as a mediator;

- The mediator assists the parties in their negotiations;

- The mediator is impartial and avoids taking sides;

- The mediation is discreet and private. You cannot use the information spoken against you in court;

- The parties are free to choose the course of action. It's an adaptable procedure;

- The mediation includes both individual conversations with the mediator and group conversations with the other party; and

The goal is to come to an agreement that will serve as a legally enforceable contract.

A non-professional, a judge, an organization (like the National Contact Point of the OECD), or an ombudsman can mediate a dispute. It's crucial to pick a mediator you can believe in and who won't have any ulterior motives.

An example: The New Nigeria Foundation

The New Nigeria Foundation, a mediator in Nigeria, has facilitated agreements between significant oil firms and regional communities. The adoption of development initiatives as a remedy for communities impacted by pollution falls under this category.

When are negotiation and mediation appropriate?

- ADR can be utilized at several times, particularly when you first become aware of an issue:

    It offers the best chance of cost savings and a speedy resolution. However, there is a chance that you won't have enough proof to be in a powerful negotiation position, and the opposing side can catch you off guard. Therefore, if you have a compelling argument and the supporting evidence is readily available, employing ADR early might be suitable. However, if you need to gather more information, it might not be.

- ADR can be used when you inform the opposing party that you want to file a lawsuit:

Before you formally present a case, you are frequently obligated to notify the opposing party. You should have more information and supporting proof at this point, and you can still wait to officially begin your case to save money and time. The "disclosure process" or waiting until you are more familiar with the opposing side's "defense" may be beneficial in some circumstances, though.

- ADR may be employed following the filing of a case but prior to the trial date:

At this point, you will have a clearer grasp of the pertinent facts, supporting evidence, and opposing side's arguments, which may make it simpler for you to get ready for ADR. However, your adversary will also be better knowledgeable about your claim. Court processes could be a useful addition to your ADR plan. For instance, you could ask for additional information and proof through disclosure that could be crucial for bargaining or mediation. The longer you wait to pursue ADR, though, the less time and money you will save as the case will already have been initiated.

Practical Tip:

The best course of action is frequently to first try negotiation or mediation (it is quicker and less expensive), but to be ready to take legal action if that fails or the agreement is not fulfilled.

In order to succeed in the ADR procedure, you must have a plan and a strategy. If you are unprepared, the opposing side might use your readiness to compromise.

10 steps to consider as you get ready for ADR

(1) Determine your goals: Choose the realistic result you want ADR to help you attain.

(2) List the main problems: Determine the topics on which the opposing side will probably differ. You'll need the strongest justifications possible for these points.

(3) Compile information and proof: Be certain of the facts of the situation and have proof to back up your version of what happened. You'll be in a stronger position to negotiate as a result.

(4) Understand the law: Although alternative dispute resolution (ADR) is not a strictly legal process, it is frequently used in situations where there is or could be a court case between the parties. Knowing the pertinent laws and how the other might be breaking them is crucial for this reason. It's crucial to be able to persuade the other party that a settlement should be reached because you will win in court.

(5) Prepare your arguments: You will be able to prepare your arguments once you are familiar with the issues, the facts, and the law. Pick your primary talking points for the discussion or mediation. These ought to be founded on the facts and the law.

(6) Recognize concessions: Settlements reached through ADR frequently include a compromise. You will frequently need to make certain compromises to aid in reaching a settlement (i.e. give things up that you want to achieve). Select the goals or issues you are willing to give ground on, and use those concessions to assist in reaching a deal that addresses your core goals and important concerns. Don't offer all of your concessions at once. Make concessions only when they are required to end a standoff and come to an agreement between the parties.

(7) Establish a minimum settlement amount or result: If you

seek compensation, identify the least amount of money you would accept in a settlement and refuse to accept a settlement that is less than this amount. However, don't agree to this minimum amount right away with the other side because you want to do more than this. Instead, think about the number since it will affect the sacrifices you feel comfortable making.

(8) Assure that a fair procedure is followed: If mediation is used, choose a neutral, trustworthy third party. Make sure the process is fair, allows you to submit your ideas and supporting facts, and permits participation from anyone you believe should be there.

(9) Hire a lawyer: It's crucial to bring a lawyer or representative from a civil society organization to the negotiation if the other side is represented by an attorney. This is essential to avoid a power disparity.

(10) Agree on all aspects with your group: If the ADR process will have an impact on a number of people, be sure that everyone is on board with the procedure's goals, justifications, concessions, and minimal amount. This will ensure that any settlement is fair.

How Do I Make a Settlement Effective?

The procedure doesn't end when an ADR settlement is reached. It's equally crucial that the other side abides by the agreement if you wish to accomplish your goals. There is no standard means of enforcement for ADR because it is an informal process. When enforcing a settlement, keep the following tactics in mind.

Making sure you establish a precise and enforceable settlement is the first step in enforcing one. If you come to a decision, carry out the following:

- Make sure the contract's terms cover the important points;

- Ascertain that both parties are aware of the practical implications of the agreement's terms;

- At the conclusion of the negotiation or mediation, document the agreement in writing; and

- Ensure the contract is signed by both parties. This is vital. The existence of a contract will be demonstrated if both parties sign the agreement.

Practical tip: Draft an action plan

The next phase is to design an action plan that aims to fix the issues brought on by the opposing party's conduct with the help of other parties involved in the case (such as nearby communities) and the opposing party. This results in the creation of a step-by-step implementation strategy for the settlement:

You can come up with an action plan, for instance, if a firm is contaminating a water source, in which case the company would agree to discontinue the actions that caused the contamination. Then, you would try to undo the harm that this pollution produced. Finally, you would pledge to take action to keep an eye on the situation and stop any further contamination. An example of this may be a plan of action for the business to protect the environment.

Try to put this in writing and get a signature on it. This might then be added as a timetable to the contract and attached to the initial agreement. If you have a legally enforceable settlement and the other party continues to break the agreement, you can sue them in court to have the settlement enforced as a contract. In the event that one side prevails, the other will likely be required to follow the terms of the agreement and, maybe, the agreed-upon action plan.

It can also be useful to get NGOs and other civil society organizations to keep an eye on how the agreement is being put into practice. If the other side doesn't carry out the agreement, they might increase awareness and apply pressure.

Create a media plan or campaign to exert pressure on the other side to carry out the agreement.

What Happens If Mediation and Negotiation Fail?

You can still file a lawsuit in court if you sought to negotiate and engage in negotiations with the opposing party but they fell through. It's not uncommon for strong individuals or organizations to try to get you to sign agreements that limit your ability to do anything but negotiate. DO NOT make a commitment of this kind.

Make sure the opposite party is aware that you would still think about filing a lawsuit if the mediation doesn't work. This may be a way to exert pressure on a more formidable opponent to engage in fruitful mediation or negotiation.

EXERCISE TO TAKE BEFORE ANY NEGOTIATION

Are you preparing for a negotiation? You might want to plan ahead. The first preparation is to consider this checklist of Negotiation Pitfalls to Avoid:

• Not Preparing Enough: Success depends on preparation.

• Assuming that the only option is for a party to lose should the other win: Instead of win-lose scenarios, seek out win-win alternatives.

• Competing Rather Than Potentially Collaborating: Determine whether there is a chance for a relationship to grow during the negotiation as opposed to competition.

• Letting Emotion Impact Your Judgment: Keep your emotions in check so they don't affect how the negotiation turns out.

• The Wrong People in the Room: Make sure all relevant parties are present for the discussion.

• Giving In to Pressure: Avoid giving in to pressure from the opposing side in the negotiation to accept a solution with which you are not happy.

• Negotiation across cultural boundaries: How business is done around the world varies. To prevent potential misunderstandings, make sure you are familiar with the cultural norms of the company you are negotiating with.

Make notes on the following points in the table below:

1. Research notes on situation/offer	
2. The absolute worst deal you'll take – and what you'll do if you don't get it. (BATNA)	
3. Prioritize what's most important to you and what you'd be willing to give up.	
4. Your counterpart's needs.	
5. Common connections you share with your counterpart(s).	
6. Identify who the stakeholders are.	
7. Where will the setting be?	
7. Do you have any	

vantage point? (state it)	
8. Does your counterpart have any weakness? (state it)	
8. What negotiation strategy(ies) do you plan to use?	

Conclusion:

With a handful of these tips, preplanning procedures, anecdotes of powerful negotiations all around the world and managing yourself as regards your emotions and decision making, you would probably never find any negotiation process daunting nor worry about getting what you want on the negotiation table. Although we aim for a win-win, but when it must be a win-lose, aim for a second best alternative nevertheless. During negotiation, do not be afraid to "play hardball" should the situation call for it, but try as much as you can to maintain solid relationships where absolutely necessary. By using the aptly termed "win-win" strategy to negotiate, you may probably come up with a desired outcome that makes everyone feel good.

www.ingramcontent.com/pod-product-compliance
Lightning Source LLC
Chambersburg PA
CBHW031626210526
45464CB00004B/1771